Editor: David Barlex

Teacher's Guide
Author: David Barlex with Jo Compton

Capability Task File
Authors: David Barlex, Terry Bendall, Torben Steeg, Paul Knapp
Illustrations: Nathan Barlex, John Plater, Torben Steeg

Addison Wesley Longman Limited
Edinburgh Gate, Harlow, Essex, CM20 2JE
© The Nuffield Foundation 1997

First published in 1997
ISBN 0 582 31770 3

Design by Linda Males
Printed by Pindar plc
Set in Minion 12/15pt

The Publishers' policy is to use paper manufactured from sustainable forests.

Contents

Part 1

Teaching D&T to 14–16 year-olds

The Nuffield approach to design and technology has proved extremely successful. At the time of writing, it is being used by over one third of the secondary schools in England and Wales. It is quite clear that the Nuffield Project's slogan, 'Teaching students to design what they are going to make and then make what they have designed' is no idle boast. These materials have been designed to build on this proven approach, but it is important to note that a school can use the materials 'from scratch' with students who have not met the approach previously. By using the approach and the associated materials, schools will be able to meet the requirements of the 1995 Statutory Orders for design and technology and prepare students for a variety of different Examination Board syllabuses. Quite deliberately, the Nuffield approach is not allied to any one Examination Board but the Nuffield Project has worked closely with a number of different Examination Boards and this guide describes how the materials can be used to meet different Examination Board requirements. The Teacher's Guide deals with the focus area of design and technology most commonly called Electronic Products. The publications for this focus area are shown below.

Electronic Products Student's Book

A complete textbook to support the students in producing course work, learning the substance of design and technology, and tackling written examinations. You will need class sets with, ideally, each student having access to their own copy.

Electronic Products Resource Tasks File

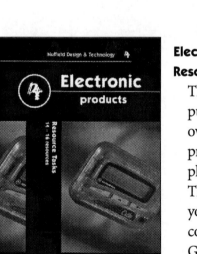

This is a once only purchase containing over 30 focused practical tasks as photocopy masters. Through these tasks you can teach the content required for GCSE success.

Electronic Products Teacher's Guide

This is a once only purchase. Part 1 explains how to use the published materials and approach to construct a scheme of work suitable for your school and Examination Board. Part 2 contains 13 different Capability Tasks.

If you teach design and technology the Nuffield way, then you will use three different teaching methods.

- **Resource Tasks** These are short practical activities. They have been designed to make students think and to help them to learn the knowledge and skill they need to design and make really well.

- **Case Studies** These are true stories about design and technology in the world outside school. By reading them, students find out more than they possibly could through designing and making alone. Through Case Studies they will learn about the way firms and businesses design and manufacture goods and how those goods are marketed and sold. They will also learn about the impact that products have on the people who use them and the places where they are made.

- **Capability Tasks** These involve designing and making a product that works. Students use what they have learned in Resource Tasks and Case Studies when they tackle a Capability Task. Capability Tasks take a lot longer than either Resource Tasks or Case Studies. You will need to organize your lessons so that students do the Resource Tasks and Case Studies they need for a Capability Task as part of that Capability Task. In this way you can make sure that your students can be successful in their designing and making.

The way these methods work together is shown here in this extract from the Student's Book.

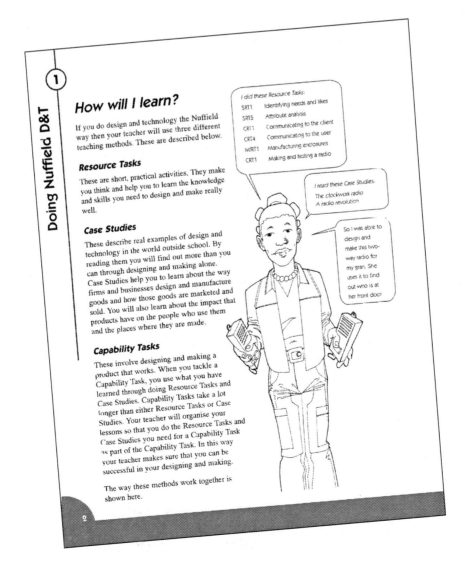

A new design for 14–16 year-olds

Each Resource Task is presented to the student as an instruction sheet, laid out like this.

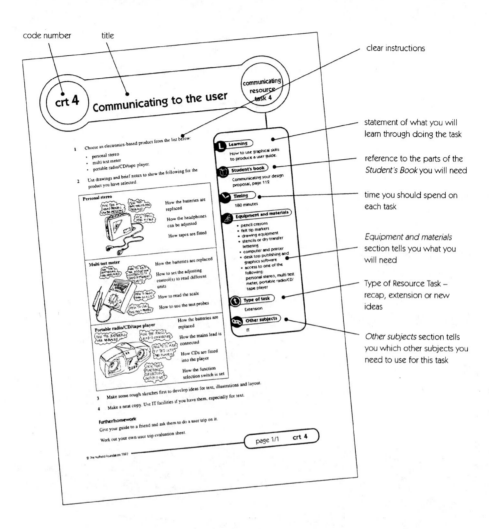

The design is different from that used earlier. While still incorporating its key features, it has two additional features appropriate for 14–16 year-olds. These are an indication of the type of task (see page 5) and the links with other subjects.

You may organize the lesson so that everyone is doing the same Resource Task, set different students different tasks or allow them to choose from a range of Resource Tasks. Sometimes the tasks require students to work on their own and sometimes as part of a team.

Chapters 4–12 of the *Electronic Products Student's Book* contain cross references to Resource Tasks as shown below, showing that the information on this page will be useful in tackling the Resource Task indicated.

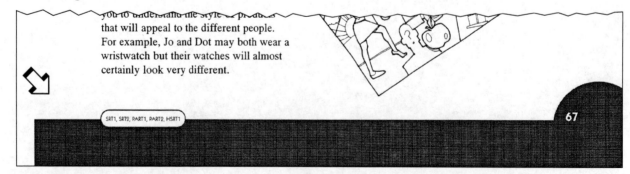

Types of Resource Task

There are three basic types of Resource Task.

- **Recapitulation Resource Tasks** These are tasks that go over things that students probably did earlier. They are very useful for reminding students of things they may have forgotten about or for catching up on things they have missed.

- **Extension Resource Tasks** These are tasks which take an idea that students were probably taught earlier and develop it further. They are useful both for revising ideas explored earlier and for helping students to use them in a more advanced way.

- **New ideas Resource Tasks** These are tasks that deal with knowledge and understanding that are new to 14–16 year-olds. It is unlikely that students will have done this sort of work before. They are important for helping the student to make progress.

You can use this classification in a number of useful ways. You can organize the sequence of Resource Tasks in a way that shows students the progress they can make by working through them. Students who are facing difficulties can spend longer on recapitulation tasks. Particularly able students can miss out recapitulation tasks altogether.

Style and range of learning through Resource Tasks

The style of learning is **active**. It always involves a response from the student. Students might have to explain, record, design, construct, investigate or test. The learning intentions for any one Resource Task are likely to be quite narrow but, where possible, tasks have been written that meet several learning intentions. In this way Resource Tasks can be used very efficiently.

Substance of Resource Tasks

The Resource Tasks are divided into 11 sets as shown in Table 1 overleaf. Five of these sets are developments of earlier Resource Tasks and there are six categories that are new for 14–16 year-olds – 'Systems boards', 'Investigation boards', 'Manufacturing', 'Components and calculations', 'Communication technology' and 'Programmable ICs'.

Through the Systems boards tasks, students will learn to use systems boards for sensing, amplifying, comparing, timing, counting and decision making. Through the Investigation boards tasks, students will investigate transistor circuits, comparators, timing circuits, logic circuits and counting. Through the Manufacturing tasks, students will learn how to produce PCBs, enclosures and electromechanical systems. Through the Components and calculations tasks, students will learn to identify components and to calculate important values. Through Communication technology tasks, students will be introduced to radio communications technology. Through the Programmable IC tasks, students will learn how to use a range of programmable ICs available in schools.

You can find a detailed summary of all the Electronic Products Resource Tasks on pages 37–40.

Table 1 – Electronic Products Resource Tasks

Strategies	Communicating	Electrics
SRT 1 Identifying needs and likes	CRT 1 Communicating ideas to the client	ECRT 1 – Controlling a simple buggy
SRT 2 Questionnaires	CRT 2 Communicating ideas to the maker 1 – construction and assembly details	ECRT 2 – Choosing batteries
SRT 3 Design briefs and specifications	CRT 3 Communicating ideas to the maker 2 – circuit diagrams, wiring diagrams, PCB layouts	
SRT 4 Brainstorming	CRT 4 Communicating to the user	
SRT 5 Attribute analysis		
SRT 6 Evaluating		
SRT 7 Systems and control		

Systems boards	Investigation boards	Manufacturing
SBRT 1 Sensing and processing with transistors	IBRT 1 Investigating transistor circuits	MfRT 1 Making circuit layouts using copper tape
SBRT 2 Using a comparator	IBRT 2 Investigating a comparator	MfRT 2 Making printed circuit boards
SBRT 3 Introducing timing into circuits	IBRT 3 Designing timing circuits	MfRT 3 Assembling an electromechanical system
SBRT 4 Combining signals	IBRT 4 Designing logic circuits	MfRT 4 Producing enclosures
SBRT 5 Circuits that count	IBRT 5 Investigating counting	

Components and calculations	Communication technology	Programmable ICs
CCRT 1 Component sorting	CTRT 1 Making and testing a radio (based on the TEP radio)	PICRT 1 Using micro controllers
CCRT 2 Resistor equations		PICRT 2 Comparing simple programmable and hard-wired systems
CCRT 3 Working with transistors and op-amps		PICRT 3 Developing sophisticated systems
CCRT 4 Capacitor equations		

Products and applications	Health and safety	
PART 1 Looking at a single product	HSRT 1 Ensuring safety in an unfamiliar situation	
PART 2 Looking at a collection of products		

Organizing the classroom

Following these guidelines will help ensure that Resource Task work is effective.

- Each student should have a copy of the instruction sheets.

- Each student should have a separate copy of any tables or worksheet required to be filled in during the task. Make sure that some spares are available for mistakes.

- Allow sufficient time and, if necessary, deviate from the recommended time.

- Ensure that the required materials, tools and equipment are readily available.

- Use a circus approach within your classroom to avoid equipment shortfalls.

- If necessary, go through the task with the class beforehand so that all students have clear targets for doing and recording.

- If necessary, demonstrate skills that will be needed in the task.

- If you require the students to tackle a sequence of Resource Tasks over successive lessons share this with the class.

- Once the students are tackling the task, support them by asking questions, giving assistance, looking at what they write and draw, helping with practical difficulties and providing encouragement.

▷ *A teacher sets up a sequence of Resource Tasks over successive lessons and goes through the first task*

The Student's Book provides support for all aspects of GCSE courses. All Student's Books have the same overall structure, ensuring continuity of treatment whatever the focus area. The purpose and key features of each section of the *Electronic Products Student's Book* are described below.

Chapter 1 Doing Nuffield D&T for 14–16 year-olds

This chapter is divided into three parts.

Part 1 Learning Design and Technology for 14–16 year-olds

This gives a clear description of the sorts of products that students will design and make during their course, plus an explanation of the Nuffield approach. The use of Resource Tasks, Capability Tasks and Case Studies is described and there is guidance on reviewing progress during a Capability Task, evaluating the final product and assessing overall progress.

Part 2 Using other subjects in D&T

This identifies ways in which students can use art, science, mathematics and information technology to enhance designing and making.

Part 3 How you will be assessed at GCSE

This gives guidance on how to develop and carry out a Capability Task for GCSE course work and how to research and write a Case Study for GCSE course work. It also describes four types of questions used for GCSE written, terminal examinations.

You can use this part of the Student's Book as the basis for whole-class teaching about the way students will learn and as a basis for helping individual students with particular difficulties. For example, you might ask a student to read the section on using science and identify some science that he or she has been taught earlier if they are tackling a Capability Task in which science is likely to be useful. This could become the basis for the student talking to both their science and D&T teachers about ways in which the science could be applied.

Chapter 2 Examination questions

A range of examination questions, approved by SCAA, and typical of those likely to be set for GCSE written, terminal examinations is presented, with comments.

Chapter 3 Case Studies

There are two sorts of Case Studies. First, there is a set that is common to all the Student's Books, whatever the focus area. These deal with the technologies which really affect the way people live. Often they are associated with a particular time in history. Reading these will help students to understand the way that technology affects our lives. Second, there are those that deal with products which are similar to those that the students will be designing and making. They will describe the following about these products:

- how the designs were developed, manufactured, marketed and sold;

- how the products work;

- how the products affect people – those who make it, those who use it and others.

A particular study may deal with just one of these or it may describe all of them. Through reading these studies, students will gain an insight into professional practice that will inform their own designing and making.

There are two devices to help students read the studies. First, 'Pause for thought' boxes which ask intriguing questions but do not require the reader to write anything down. They are there to provide motivation to read more. Second, there are 'Questions' boxes. You can use these as staging posts for reading a Case Study as a class activity. For example, you could instruct the class as follows: 'I want you to spend 15 minutes reading this Case Study and discussing the questions with your partner. Then I want you to answer the questions in writing. This should take you a further 10 minutes.' The Case Studies also contain 'Research activity'. You can set these for homework as they involve finding information that is not in the Case Study.

The titles of the Case Studies are shown in Table 2. You can find details of their links to Capability Tasks in the Capability Task Summary Tables on pages 42–45.

Table 2 – Electronic Products Case Studies

General Case Studies	Focused Case Studies
Public transport in London	Sensing devices – joist/wiring detector
DIY medical testing	Measuring devices – excercise cycle
Information – the power to change lives	Electronic novelties – 'soft' noise making toys
Designing our surroundings	Security devices – intruder alarms for cars
	Communicating devices – clockwork radio
	Communicating devices – bus arrival times system, the countdown service
	Electronic load controllers for micro hydro power
	Helping to keep air breathable
	A radio revolution

Chapter 4 Strategies for designing

This chapter revisits and develops strategies from earlier work and introduces some new strategies for 14–16 year-olds. The strategies are shown in Table 3. The aim of this chapter is to provide the student with a repertoire of strategies and sufficient understanding to be able to choose and use them appropriately.

Table 3 – Strategies for 14–16 year-olds

Strategies	Strategies
Identifying needs and likes	Applying science
PIES	choice of materials
observing people	Systems thinking
asking questions	input, process, outputs
using books and magazines	subsystems, boundaries, interfaces
image boards	feedback and control
questionnaires	Planning
Design briefs	Gantt charts
Specifications	flow charts
Generating design ideas	Evaluating
brainstorming	user trip
attribute analysis	winners and losers
observational drawing	performance testing
investigative drawing	appropriateness
Modelling	
modelling appearance	
modelling performance	
modelling with computers	

Chapter 5 Communicating design proposals

This chapter builds on the earlier approach in detailing the techniques used by designers to communicate with clients, manufacturers and users. The aim of this chapter is to enable the student to choose and use techniques that are appropriate for the information to be conveyed. Table 4 summarizes the techniques and purposes dealt with in this chapter.

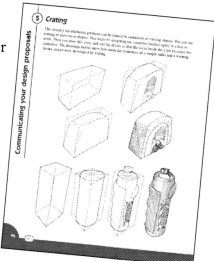

Table 4 – Communication techniques for 14–16 year-olds

What you want to communicate	Techniques or drawing systems to use
realistic appearance of a product	rendering on perspective or isometric views
overall appearance with correct proportion	crating
scale drawing suitable for CAD	isometric drawing
cost of materials and components	costing chart
details for making the container	orthographic projection
details of the circuit	circuit diagram
details of circuit construction	PCB layout diagram
internal details	sectional views
how parts fit together	exploded views
special features	hidden detail animation for moving parts enlarged detail

Chapter 6 Design guides

The Nuffield Project has developed the idea of a line of interest as a means of limiting the sort of product that students in a class might design and make. This makes the teaching of a Capability Task much more manageable. A line of interest describes a particular type of product and the Nuffield Project has suggested the following six individual lines of interest as being suitable for Electronic Products:

- sensing devices
- measuring devices
- electronic novelties
- security devices
- control systems
- communicating devices.

Chapter 6 contains general design guides for inputs, outputs, enclosures, user interfaces and quality, plus specific design guides for each of the lines of interest. Each of the specific guides deals with the issues that should be considered when designing within this line of interest. They set an agenda for the students, rather than providing the answers. The design guides provide a

Using the Student's Book

11

straightforward way for students to become familiar with areas of electronic design. They can act as a stimulus for students who are having difficulty in deciding on their main coursework. They can provide a reminder during a Capability Task to ensure that important issues are not overlooked. You can use the design guides in a number of ways.

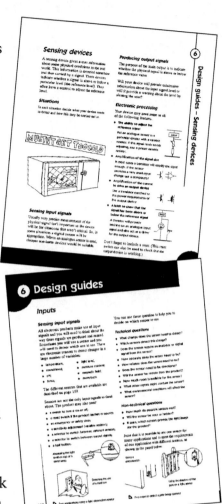

- In one-to-one conversations with individual students, as in: 'I'm not sure that you've thought about all the important things here; let's look at the design guide to see if you've missed anything.'

- In conversations with small groups, as in: 'I want you to use the design guide to find four questions to ask each other about your design ideas. I'll be back in ten minutes to see how you're getting on.'

- In a question and answer session with the whole class, as in: 'It says here that electronic products make use of input signals and that these are sometimes sensed. OK, Jane, I want you to tell the class three sorts of things that an electronic product might sense. Then, Paul, I want you to tell me how the product might sense these things.'

- As a reading homework in preparation for a Capability Task which you can build on with a question and answer session during the following lesson.

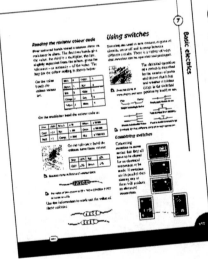

Chapter 7 Basic electrics

This chapter revises the basics established in earlier work – component symbols, circuit diagrams, series and parallel circuits, and different types of switch. It looks more closely at different types of light source, the resistor colour code, the use of protective resistors and ways of controlling electric motors. It finishes with a discussion of batteries.

Chapter 8 Basic mechanics

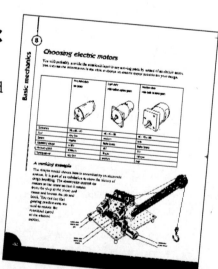

This chapter revises and extends the overview of mechanisms established in earler work by presenting a Chooser Chart for mechanisms that give a variety of outputs from a rotational input, a Chooser Chart describing electric motors, and an example of an exhibition model using both mechanical and electrical systems.

Chapter 9 Electronic devices as systems

This chapter revises and extends the systems approach introduced earlier and details the following topics, using a systems board approach:

- understanding system diagrams
- using system boards
- electronic signals
- designing electronic systems
    - inputs
    - outputs
    - process
- using transistors
- the comparator
- electronic timing
- electronic counting
    - binary, decimal and hexadecimal numbering systems
- digital logic
    - inverters
    - bistables
    - truth tables for AND, NAND, OR, NOR, and XOR gates
    - analogue processing.

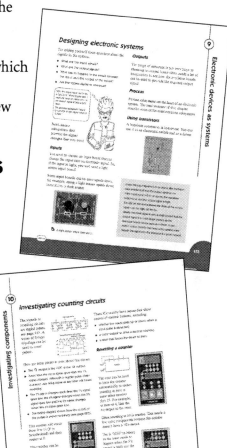

The equipment examples throughout this chapter are the Alpha boards supplied by Unilab (Lynn Lane, Shenstone, Lichfield, Staffordshire, WS14 0EE – 01543 483064).

The chapter closes with a Subsystems Chooser Chart which describes the systems boards available in the Alpha kit. Students can use this Chooser Chart to get a rapid overview of the possibilities afforded by this approach.

Chapter 10 Investigating components

This chapter revises and extends the understanding of components introduced earlier and details the following topics using an investigations board approach:

- investigating transistors
    - transistor as a switch
    - transistor as a voltage amplifier and inverter
    - transistor as a current amplifier
- thyristors
- investigating comparators
    - voltage amplification
    - analogue to digital signal conversion
    - comparing signals from two sensors
- investigating timing circuits
    - resistor capacitor networks
    - timer ICs
    - 555 monostable
    - 555 astable
    - 555 bistable
- investigating logic circuits
    - combinational logic
    - sequential logic
- investigating counting circuits
    - D-type flip-flops
    - resetting a counter.

The equipment examples throughout this chapter are the investigation boards supplied by Economatics (Education) Ltd (Epic House, Darnall Road, Attercliff, Sheffield, S9 5AA – 01142 813344).

Chapter 11 Monitoring signals

This chapter describes in detail the following different measurements that students can make on electronic signals:

- measuring voltage
    voltage measurement checklist
- measuring current
    current measurement checklist
- reading analogue scales
- monitoring signals
    using a multimeter
    multimeter checklist
    reading digital scales
    measuring resistance

- component testing
    using an ohmmeter
- measuring signals in systems
    digital signals
    using an oscilloscope
    oscilloscope checklist
- signal generators
- computer datalogging

The chapter closes with a Measurement Chooser Chart which summarizes possible measurement methods. Students can use this Chooser Chart to decide on appropriate methods.

Chapter 12 Component information

This chapter presents information about components as a series of Chooser Charts which students can use to make decisions about the components they need for the electronic system they have designed. The Chooser Charts presented are summarized in Table 5 below.

Table 5 – Chooser Charts

Power supplies Chooser Chart	Resistors Chooser Chart	Capacitors Chooser Chart
batteries and cells	fixed resistors	low capacitance (non-electrolytic)
battery holders	variable resistors	high capacitance (electrolytic)
solar cells	knobs	for tuning (variable non-electrolytic)
lead acid battery	**Diodes Chooser Chart**	**Connectors Chooser Chart**
hand generator		
low-voltage supply	steering signals	temporary
calculating with power supplies	recitifying ac	semi-permanent
	protecting other components	multiple line

Switches Chooser Chart	Sensors Chooser Chart	Output transducers Chooser Chart
electrical characteristics	For detecting the following (sensors may be	illumination
physical characteristics	digital or analogue and need not be linear):	indication
Processes Chooser Chart	• magnetism, • proximity (without touching)	distance signalling
	• visible light, • infra red, • heat,	rotary motion
transistors	• liquid level, • turning, • linear motion,	linear motion
Darlington pair	• force, • time, • sound	sound
thyristors:	For measuring the following (requires analogue	electrical switching
operational amplifiers (op-amps)	sensors, preferably with linear outputs):	fluid control
analogue to digital conversion	• visible light, • infra red, • temperature,	magnetism
digital integrated circuits	• humidity, • liquid level, • motion, rotary,	display of numbers or letters
	• motion, linear, • sound, • force	

Equations Chooser Chart		
The final Chooser Chart deals with choosing equation for calculations and contains worked examples for the following:		
Ohm's law	power equation	transistor gain
combining resistors	combining capacitors	op-amp gain
potential divider	time delays with resistors and capacitors	

Chapter 13 Using radio technology

The aim of this chapter is to provide an introduction to an area of electronics which is prevalent in everyday life and can provide interesting opportunities for major project work. The following features are described:

- radio waves
- sound waves
- transmission and reception
- modulation
- FM radio circuit (based on the TEP radio)
- radio control.

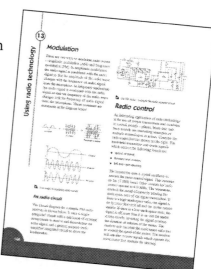

Chapter 14 Programmable ICs

The aim of this chapter is to provide an introduction to this important and rapidly developing area of control technology. The following features are described and it is important to note that programmable ICs can be used with extreme effectiveness in major projects:

- microprocessors
- micro controllers
- micro controllers in industry
- creating a program
- testing a programme
    simulation
    computer control
    EPROM
- product opportunities

Chapter 15 Making the product

This chapter is divided into two sections.

1 Electronic assembly

This section describes the following techniques required to produce the electronic working of the product:

- temporary connections
- permanent connections
- printed circuit boards
    designing a PCB
    making a PCB
    putting components in place
    being systematic
- finding faults
- surface mounting components.

2 Making the container

Information about materials

This is presented as a Chooser Chart. The following materials are included:

- jelutong
- pine
- medium density fibre board
- plywood
- aluminium sheet/tubing
- steel sheet
- high impact polystyrene sheet
- acrylic sheet
- butyrate tubing
- PVC tubing.

They are described in terms of the following features:

- description
- thermal conductivity
- electrical conductivity
- cost
- environmental audit
- availability
- applications.

Students can use this Materials Chooser Chart to select materials for electronic products.

Making your own enclosure

This describes the following techniques required to produce the final product:

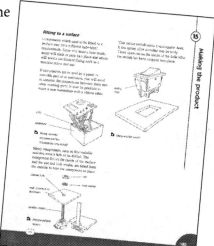

- assembling from tubing and end caps
- assembling from flat pieces
- drape forming acrylic sheet
- line bending acrylic sheet
- assembling from shaped pieces of different materials
- forming from a single sheet of metal
- forming from a sheet of thermoplastic material
- forming more complex shapes
- fitting to a surface
- fitting things inside
- buying in.

The aim of *Electronic assembly* and *Making the container* is to provide students with the information necessary to choose the most appropriate making process and the correct tools when they are making their products. Clearly, the information will not impart the tacit know-how required to use tools safely and effectively. There is no substitute for clear skill instruction and the opportunity to practise, so it is important that you use sound demonstration linked to appropriate Resource Tasks to enable students to increase their making skills.

Chapter 16 Health & Safety

This chapter revisits some important ideas established in earlier work – hazards, risks, risk assessment and risk control – and uses them to look at safety in the workplace.

Specifying a Capability Task

The Nuffield Project has identified the following 14 features which should be explained in order to describe a Capability Task and the associated learning for 14–16 year-olds. It is based on the successful model used earlier but five of the features are new.

1 **The task** A short statement which indicates the type of product the students will design and make.

2 **Task setting** It is important that the task is placed in a setting that can be investigated in a way that informs the subsequent designing and making. The investigation should answer the following questions.

- Who is the product for?

- What is it for?

- Where will it be used?

- When will it be used?

- Is it a one-off or to be mass produced?

- Where might it be sold?

- Who is likely to buy it?

3 **Aims** These will indicate what is to be taught through the task. This will be linked to the type of product that the students will design and make and usually includes four features:

- learning and using some strategies

- learning and using some technical knowledge and understanding

- learning and using some communication techniques

- learning and using some making skills.

4 **Values** It is important for students to appreciate the values that inform the nature of the need or opportunity and to find ways to take them into account. This is more complex than features **5** and **6** as the detail of the value considerations will depend on the nature of the task setting. This will be revealed by the students' investigation of the setting and for this they will need appropriate strategies. These will be detailed in a programme of study or syllabus and can be taught through an appropriate set or sequence of Resource Tasks (see feature **9**). It will be important for students to consider their own values and move towards a recognition and understanding of the values of others. They will need to think about situations where there are value conflicts and move from simple two-sided arguments to understanding complex conflicts involving many-sided arguments. Arguments where qualitative values, such as aesthetic considerations, are in conflict with quantitative values, such as economic considerations, are probably the most difficult to resolve. The values are presented under the following headings:

- technical • economic • aesthetic • moral • social • environmental.

They do not represent mutually exclusive sets and there will often be overlaps between the categories. Reading and thinking about Case Studies is a useful way to develop values thinking (see **10**).

5 **Nature of the product** This will describe the sort of product that the students will design and make at a level of detail that indicates the knowledge, understanding and skills likely to be required. For example, a sensing device which sounds an alarm when the temperature drops below a particular level is a simple product even with an vacuum-formed case and user guide. Designing and making this is a modest task. A measuring device which senses the temperature at four different locations and displays their value on a series of led bar graphs held on a vacuum-formed monitor at a central location and sounds an alarm when any three of these detect a temperature below a particular level is a much more demanding affair. There is a dynamic relationship between the nature of the product and the knowledge and understanding of technical matters and making skill. Complex products *demand* high level knowledge and skill; high level knowledge and skill *lead* to complex products.

6 **Technical knowledge and understanding** This is related to the nature of the product which the students are designing and making and can be cross-referenced against the programme of study or syllabus and taught through an appropriate set or sequence of Resource Tasks (see feature **9**).

7 **Specialist tools, equipment and materials** For 14–16 year-olds it is assumed that most general-purpose hand tools and light machine tools will be available. Only specialist or unusual items will be noted. Similarly, with materials, fixings and fittings, only the uncommon will be detailed. Suitable suppliers will also be indicated.

8 **Cross-curricular links** The use of other areas of knowledge and understanding should be such that they aid the students' designing and making. The approach of, say, science to a particular area (such as understanding the electromagnetic spectrum) will not necessarily generate understanding that is applicable in a design and technology task. Using an RF meter to detect the signal from a transmitter circuit and tuning the frequency of transmission by adjusting the core of the coils is a very different task to learning about the applications of radio waves as part of work on the electromagnetic spectrum. However, a different approach by the design and technology teacher, concentrating perhaps on practical application rather than an underlying explanation, may only serve to confuse the student further. So it will be important to check with colleagues in other curriculum areas and to try to use a consistent approach even though it will be for different purposes.

The cross-curricular links are summarized using headings which indicate a particular subject or theme, such as using art or using economic and industrial understanding.

9 **Useful Resource Tasks** A listing of relevant Resource Tasks is always provided. Only you will know which ones are appropriate for your students. Depending on their previous experience and learning, they may need to do all of the suggested tasks, some or only a few. In a very few cases, a student may not need to do any but this is likely to be a rare exception as an important feature of capability is the ability to use new knowledge, understanding and skills.

10 **Useful Case Studies** A listing of relevant Case Studies is always provided. Only you will know which ones are appropriate for your students or how best to use them – with the whole class, with a small group or with an individual. They do provide an important opportunity for the student to reflect on the wider issues of design and technology as well as more focused work concerning quality, products and applications.

A clear description of features **1–10** above provides a detailed specification for a Capability Task. This whole approach makes it clear what you have to teach for students to become capable in design and technology. It is only when the teaching requirements are clear that you can organize lessons so that learning can take place. However, in order to enable you to modify the tasks and start them at different points from usual (see page 22), the following features are also described.

11 Design brief This will always describe the following features:

- the sort of product that is to be made and its purpose

- who will use it

- where it will be used

- where it might be sold.

12 Preliminary specification This will always describe the following features:

- what it should do

- what it should look like

- other features, such as:
  - how it should work
  - how much it should cost to manufacture – or limiting cost of starting materials
  - possible production levels, such as one off or batch
  - from what materials it should be made
  - what energy source should be used
  - ergonomic requirements related to end user
  - legal requirements to be met in its development
  - environmental considerations and requirements.

13 Design sketches These will give an impression of one or two products that could be made in response to the brief and specification. There will be insufficient information for the student to make the product without more design input. A systems block diagram for a possible solution will also be presented.

14 Information for making These will deal with simple, rather than complex, products. They will usually include the following:

- a description of a likely and basic solution to the task

- an appropriate circuit diagram

- an appropriate PCB mask

- details of a simple enclosure

- suggestions for modifying the circuit

- suggestions for improving the enclosure.

⑤ How the Capability Tasks are presented

Capability Tasks for 14–16 year-olds are presented as two, three or four copymaster A4 overview sheets so that the information is easily and rapidly accessible.

Title

Line of interest

Task

Task setting

Aims of the task

Specialist tools, equipment and materials

Value considerations

Nature of the product students will produce

Technical knowledge and understanding

Cross-curricular links

Relevant Resource Tasks

Relevant Case Studies

Design brief

Specification

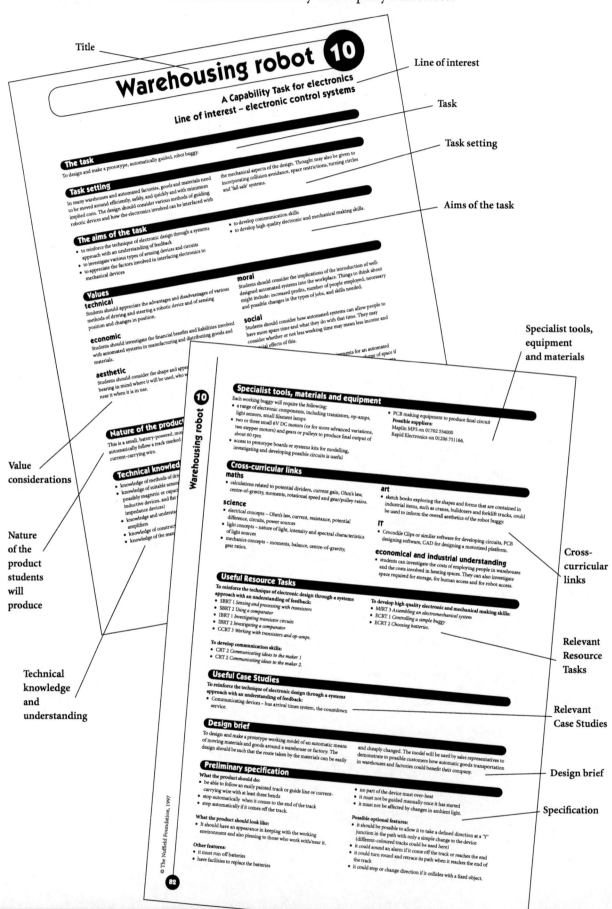

Warehousing robot ⑩

A Capability Task for electronics
Line of interest – electronic control systems

The task
To design and make a prototype, automatically guided, robot buggy.

Task setting
In many warehouses and automated factories, goods and materials need to be moved around efficiently, safely, and quickly and with minimum implied costs. The design should consider various methods of guiding robotic devices and how the electronics involved can be interfaced with the mechanical aspects of the design. Thought may also be given to incorporating collision avoidance, space restrictions, turning circles and 'fail safe' systems.

The aims of the task
- to reinforce the technique of electronic design through a systems approach with an understanding of feedback
- to investigate various types of sensing devices and circuits
- to appreciate the factors involved in interfacing electronics to mechanical devices
- to develop communication skills
- to develop high quality electronic and mechanical making skills.

Values
technical
Students should appreciate the advantages and disadvantages of various methods of driving and steering a robotic device and of sensing position and changes in position.

economic
Students should investigate the financial benefits and liabilities involved with automated systems in manufacturing and distributing goods and materials.

aesthetic
Students should consider the shape and appe... bearing in mind where it will be used, who w... near it when it is in use.

moral
Students should consider the implications of the introduction of well-designed automated systems into the workplace. Things to think about might include: increased profits, number of people employed, necessary and possible changes in the types of jobs, and skills needed.

social
Students should consider how automated systems can allow people to have more spare time and what they do with that time. They may consider whether or not less working time may mean less income and ... al effects of this.

Nature of the product
This is a small, battery-powered, mo... automatically follow a track marked ... current-carrying wire.

Technical knowled...
- knowledge of methods of dri...
- knowledge of suitable senso... possibly magnetic or capaci... inductive devices, and flat ... impedance devices)
- knowledge and understa... amplifiers
- knowledge of construct...
- knowledge of the ma...

Specialist tools, materials and equipment
Each working buggy will require the following:
- a range of electronic components, including transistors, op-amps, light sensors, small filament lamps
- two or three small 6V DC motors (or for more advanced variations, two stepper motors) and gears or pulleys to produce final output of about 60 rpm
- access to prototype boards or systems kits for modelling, investigating and developing possible circuits is useful
- PCB making equipment to produce final circuit

Possible suppliers:
Maplin MPS on 01702 554000
Rapid Electronics on 01206 751166.

Cross-curricular links
maths
- calculations related to potential dividers, current gain, Ohm's law, centre-of-gravity, moments, rotational speed and gear/pulley ratios.

science
- electrical concepts – Ohm's law, current, resistance, potential difference, circuits, power sources
- light concepts – nature of light, intensity and spectral characteristics of light sources
- mechanics concepts – moments, balance, centre-of-gravity, gear ratios.

art
- sketch books exploring the shapes and forms that are contained in industrial items, such as cranes, bulldozers and forklift trucks, could be used to inform the overall aesthetics of the robot buggy.

IT
- Crocodile Clips or similar software for developing circuits, PCB designing software, CAD for designing a motorized platform.

economical and industrial understanding
- students can investigate the costs of employing people in warehouses and the costs involved in heating spaces. They can also investigate space required for storage, for human access and for robot access.

Useful Resource Tasks
To reinforce the technique of electronic design through a systems approach with an understanding of feedback:
- SBRT 1 *Sensing and processing with transistors*
- SBRT 2 *Using a comparator*
- IBRT 1 *Investigating transistor circuits*
- IBRT 2 *Investigating a comparator*
- CCRT 3 *Working with transistors and op-amps.*

To develop communication skills:
- CRT 2 *Communicating ideas to the maker 1*
- CRT 2 *Communicating ideas to the maker 2.*

To develop high quality electronic and mechanical making skills:
- MfRT 3 *Assembling an electromechanical system*
- ECRT 1 *Controlling a simple buggy*
- ECRT 2 *Choosing batteries.*

Useful Case Studies
To reinforce the technique of electronic design through a systems approach with an understanding of feedback:
- Communicating devices – bus arrival times system, the countdown service.

Design brief
To design and make a prototype working model of an automatic means of moving materials and goods around a warehouse or factory. The design should be such that the route taken by the materials can be easily and cheaply changed. The model will be used by sales representatives to demonstrate to possible customers how automatic goods transportation in warehouses and factories could benefit their company.

Preliminary specification
What the product should do:
- be able to follow an easily painted track or guide line or current-carrying wire with at least three bends
- stop automatically when it comes to the end of the track
- stop automatically if it comes off the track.

What the product should look like:
- It should have an appearance in keeping with the working environment and also pleasing to those who work with/near it.

Other features:
- it must run off batteries
- have facilities to replace the batteries

- no part of the device must over-heat
- it must not be guided manually once it has started
- it must not be affected by changes in ambient light.

Possible optional features:
- it should be possible to allow it to take a defined direction at a 'Y' junction in the path with only a simple change to the device (different-coloured tracks could be used here)
- it could sound an alarm if it come off the track or reaches the end
- it could turn round and retrace its path when it reaches the end of the track
- it could stop or change direction if it collides with a fixed object.

© The Nuffield Foundation, 1997

82

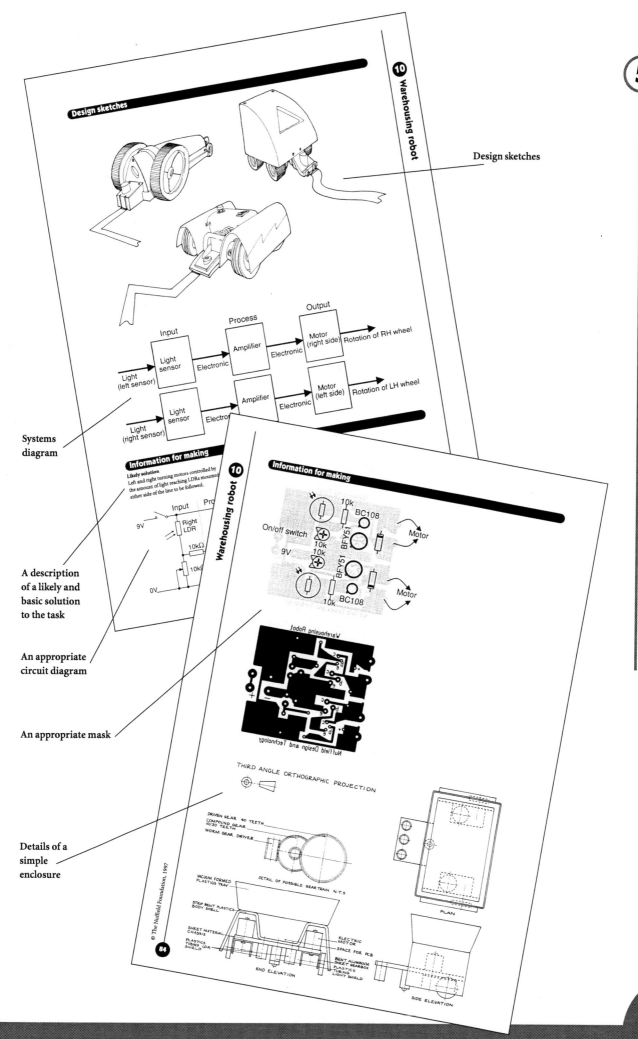

Design sketches

Systems diagram

A description of a likely and basic solution to the task

An appropriate circuit diagram

An appropriate mask

Details of a simple enclosure

Design sketches

Warehousing robot 10

Information for making

Likely solution
Left and right turning motors controlled by the amount of light reaching LDRs mounted either side of the line to be followed.

THIRD ANGLE ORTHOGRAPHIC PROJECTION

© The Nuffield Foundation, 1997

5 Using the Capability Tasks to plan a full GCSE course

Managing three Capability Tasks

It is likely that your students will tackle three Capability Tasks during year 10, each one from a different line of interest. You can work out which ones your class will tackle. In year 11 students can revisit a line of interest or tackle a new one. The one in year 11 will probably be the one that is used for their GCSE course work. This makes sense because the students should be better at designing and making in year 11 than they were in year 10. It will be quite a struggle to fit three complete Capability Tasks into year 10 so you may wish to organize the lessons so that students do only part of some of these tasks. They will certainly need to do one complete Capability Task where they design, make and test a well-finished product. There are several ways to shorten Capability Tasks.

- You might shorten it so that the students produce only a working model or collection of models of the product. This means that the time spent is reduced as the students don't have to spend a lot of time making the finished article.

- You might decide that the students should produce only a series of design proposals as detailed annotated sketches. This cuts down the time they spend on the Capability Task even further.

- You may decide to give the class a design brief plus a specification and ask them to design and make a product that meets these requirements. This removes all of the task setting investigation from the task, brief and specification development and so lessens the time spent.

- You could decide to give the class the brief, specification and some design sketches as a starting point. This will cut down the design development phase even further.

- You might even give the class the brief, the specification and the information for making and ask them to make the product because, for example, they need to concentrate on manufacturing. This will reduce the time spent even further.

Example briefs, specifications, design sketches and information for making are included in the Capability Task File so that you have control over the time spent on the tasks. Of course, it is important that the students still carry out the Resource Tasks and Case Studies needed for each of the Capability Tasks. In this way they can acquire lots of design and technology knowledge, understanding and skill and still keep in touch with designing and making. This will put the students in a strong position to tackle a full Capability Task in year 11. Of course, it is important that the students know at the outset of the Capability Task how long it is going to take and in what way it will be shortened from being a full Capability Task. They need to be quite clear as to the expected outcomes. There is little that is more disappointing for a student than to start a Capability Task with the expectation of taking home a finished piece only to be told during the task: 'Well we haven't got time to finish so your systems diagram and breadboard circuit will have to do.'

Short course requirements

If you are teaching a short course you will need to reduce the number of Capability Tasks accordingly and perhaps complete just one full and one reduced-time task before students tackle their main task for GCSE assessment.

Choosing the lines of interest

The lines of interest have been chosen because they represent different degrees of risk as far as the teacher is concerned. Some of the lines of interest involve students designing and making products with which most teachers are quite familiar and the likelihood of the students being successful is high. This is simply because the teacher is so familiar with the knowledge, understanding and skill required for success, and the typical pitfalls, that he or she can teach appropriately to the task and provide effective guidance without the student losing ownership of the work. Other lines of interest are slightly less safe and the majority of teachers may feel some concern about the level of success they can guarantee with students designing and making these sorts of product. Some other lines of interest may be seen as high risk in that they are outside the previous experience of the teacher. Exactly what constitutes a risk to you and the level of that risk will depend on your specialist training, any in-service training you may have received, the facilities in your school and your previous teaching experience. So while only you can make the best judgement the Nuffield Project does offer this guidance. Of the three Capability Tasks you might teach in year 10, choose two that are low risk. In this way the bulk of your work in year 10 is likely to be successful. If, for some reason, you are not successful in this area of risk then the damage is easy to limit. If, however, you are successful, this is good professional development and, over a period of time, this part of your teaching will cease to be one of risk and become an area of guaranteed success. You will then be in a position to tackle a further and different area of risk in the knowledge that you can be successful.

In-built assessment through reviewing

It is important that your students work in a way that reveals their design and technology thinking. Evidence of their capability should emerge quite naturally from the way they tackle a Capability Task. The way that students review the progress of their work during a Capability Task is an important means of providing you with assessment evidence. From the students' view point, reviewing is essential for two reasons. First, it demands that the students stop and reflect on what they have done so far and the consequences of this for further action. Thus it is an important strategy in giving students a sense that designing is a coherent and continuous activity; that the activity is not a series of unconnected steps prompted, perhaps, by teacher intervention or worksheet instruction. It is important for the student to view designing as a sequence of connected activities over which they have some control. Reviewing helps to establish this view. Second, in confronting students with the consequences of their actions the review procedure can provide momentum for the task in that it forces students to make decisions about what to do next.

In one sense, reviewing should be happening continuously as every action should be the result of a plan-execute-review cycle:
- 'I plan to take a particular cause of action because …'
- 'I do it.'
- 'I reflect on the result of the doing (that is, I review the consequences of my actions) and use these thoughts to plan my next action' and so on.

It is quite impossible to monitor this continuous and on-going reviewing within a student's work but the Nuffield Project has identified the following three staging posts in design activity where a more formal review is extremely useful.

First review

Once students have some ideas for their products in the form of quickly drawn, annotated sketches and rough systems diagrams, they should carry out their first review by comparing their ideas with the requirements of the brief and the specification. They should ask themselves the following questions for each design idea.
- Will the design do what it is supposed to?
- Will the design be suitable for the users?
- Will the design fit in with where it might be used or sold?
- Is the design likely to work?
- Does the design look right for the users and sellers?
- Have I noted any special requirements the design will need to meet later on?

Any design ideas that do not get a 'yes' for all these questions will need to be rejected or adjusted. In this way the students can use the first review to screen out any design ideas that will not meet their requirements. They can do this screening in two ways:
- as an individual, by just sitting, thinking it through in their heads and making notes against each design idea
- they can work in a group and explain their ideas to other students who can check them out against the questions.

The latter method takes longer and each student has to help the others in the group to check out their design ideas, but the extra time is usually well spent as the overall level of constructive criticism is higher. Which ever way you choose for your students to review their work, it is important that they discuss their review findings with you.

Second review

By screening their early ideas, students will be able to focus their efforts into developing a single design idea and then work out the details of that design. They will present these details as a mixture of circuit diagrams, simple models, rendered drawings and working drawings (sometimes called plans) which will include pcb layout drawings.

To make sure that their designing is still developing in a sensible direction, they need to ask the following questions before they begin making the product.

- Am I sure that the working parts of the design will do what they are supposed to?
- Am I sure about the accuracy with which I need to make each part?
- How long will it take me to make and assemble all the parts of my design?
- Have I got enough time to do this?
- If not, what can I alter so that I have a design which I can make on time and which still meets the specification?
- Will the materials I need be available when I need them?
- Will the tools and equipment be available when I need them?
- Am I sure that I can get the final appearance that I need?
- Have I got enough time for finishing?
- Is there anything I can do to make my working more efficient?

The individual student is probably the only one who can answer these questions but it is important that you establish the routine whereby they check their answers with you in order to avoid hidden traps and pitfalls.

Third review

Once the design has been produced, each student should review their product to check performance against specification, user reaction, winner/loser balance and appropriateness. There are Resource Tasks which revise these methods of evaluation and it is important to make these product-evaluation sessions active. One way to do this is for you to organize students into discussion groups. Each student gives their product a blob score for each part of the specification – five blobs if it meets that part really well, three blobs if it meets it moderately well, one blob if it meets it only poorly and no blobs if it fails to meet this part of the specification. Each student, in turn, then explains to the other students in the group why these scores have been given. The rest of the group questions these judgements. Each student has to convince the others that the judgements are correct. This activity is a powerful precursor to looking at overall progress.

Students looking at their own progress

At the end of a Capability Task it is important for students to look back at what they have done and reflect on their progress. The Student's Book contains the following sets of questions to help students to do this.

Feeling good about what you have done

- Am I proud of what I have made?
- Can I explain why?
- Am I proud of the design I developed?
- Can I explain why?

Understanding the problems

- What sort of things slowed me down?
- Can I now see how to overcome these sorts of difficulty?
- What sort of things made me nervous so that I didn't do as well as I know I can?

Assessment

- Do I know where to get help now?
- What sort of things did I do better than I expected?
- Was this due to luck or can I say that I'm getting better?
- Were there times when I concentrated on detail before I had the broad picture?
- Were there times when I didn't bother enough with detail?
- Can I now see how to get the level of detail right?

Understanding yourself

- Were there times when I lost interest?
- Can I now see how to get myself motivated?
- Were there times when I couldn't work out what to do next?
- Can I now see how to get better at making decisions?
- Were there times when I lost my sense of direction?
- Can I now see how to avoid this?

Understanding your design decisions

- With hindsight, can I see where I made the right decisions?
- With hindsight, can I see where I should have made different decisions?
- With hindsight, can I see situations where I did the right thing?
- With hindsight, can I see where I would do things differently if I did this again?

You can use students' answers to these questions to see strengths and weaknesses and to identify areas for improvement.

Examination questions

The Nuffield Project has identified eight types of questions which may be set for GCSE written, terminal examinations. It is important that you are familiar with these and teach your students to respond appropriately to each type.

Type 1: knowledge definitions

The candidate is expected to show understanding of key terms, principles and concepts. The question will be written in a form which requires candidates to *recognize* or *give an example* which illustrates the meaning, but does not expect candidates to be able to recall and state a definition.

Example

A local small business, called Electric Fun, specializes in electronic novelty products and has asked you to suggest some product ideas for their new catalogue. They want products that will *appeal* to mail order customers.

For recognition

Imagine you are writing a questionnaire to check which of your four product ideas is most *appealing*. Which of the following questions would you include?

- Which product looks most fun?
- Which product would 'Electric Fun' like best?
- Which product would you buy?
- Which product do you like?

For giving examples

Imagine you need to write a questionnaire to check which of your four product ideas is most *appealing*. Suggest three suitable questions.

Both of these aspects could be extended to ask students to *explain* their choices and to describe *methods* of carrying out the survey and collecting and presenting results.

Type 2: knowledge of purpose (Why?)

The candidate is expected to show understanding of:
- why things are done in a particular way ('Why do it in that way?')
- why actions or decisions are significant or important ('Why would you do x?' or 'Why is it like that?')
- why decisions are appropriate or have been made ('Why has it been made from x?').
The question will be written in a form which asks the student to explain or justify something.

Example

The candidate will be given information about a product in the form of annotated illustrations and text. They will be asked to explain different features of the design, such as:
- why a particular component has been chosen
- why a part is the shape and form that it is.
This could be extended to ask students to explain the *methods* they used or to *predict* the effects of changed variables or to make a *creative response*.

Type 3: knowledge of method (How?)

The candidate is expected to describe or explain, showing an understanding of:
- processes, materials and techniques ('How could I make this design from particular materials?')
- the application of technological principles ('Show how you would do x or make x happen')
- the application of design strategies ('How would you research, analyse, review, make decisions, plan, test, evaluate, etc.').
The question will be written in a form which asks students to *describe* using a suitable mode of response, such as notes and diagrams, grid/matrix or flow chart etc.

Example

The candidate will be given information about a product in the form of annotated illustrations and text and asked:
- how particular parts might be manufactured
- how risks can be avoided when using a necessary technique
- for a circuit, how particular components (or subsystems) work together to provide the required output from the input
- how the product could be adapted to make it easier to use
- how to test a particular part for weather resistance
- how to carry out a user trip
- how to calculate costs of making.

Type 4: speculating about change (What if?)

The candidate will be asked to predict the results of given changes in circumstances or variables, including:
- the direct consequences of things ('What would happen if you did x?')
- the effect on connected things ('If you changed x, what effect would this have on y?').
The question will be written in a form which asks the student to *suggest what would happen if...*

Example

The candidate will be presented with a diagram showing the layout and dimensions of printed circuit boards to be produced from stock UV-sensitive PCB board 0.75 m x 0.5 m.

Consider a direct consequence

You could not get the PCB board in 0.75 m x 0.5 m sheets; it is only available in a 0.5 m x 0.5 m squares.

- Say whether you will need more or less PCB board and show how you worked out your answer.

Consider an indirect consequence

You have decided to use a thyristor instead of a relay in the latching circuit.

- List the main stages needed to produce the original printed circuit board.
- Then show how this plan would change.

Type 5: creative problem-solving

The candidate will be asked to develop a *personal response* to a short technical design problem. The question will be written in a form which requires students to *suggest* possible solutions, *compare* their alternatives and select and *justify a recommended* solution.

Example

The candidate will be presented with an incomplete design to which there are several different possible solutions. Three tasks might then be asked of them, such as:

- use notes and sketches to illustrate two possible solutions to the problem
- make a list for each of your ideas to show the strengths and weaknesses of your solutions
- state clearly which idea you think is the best and give your reasons.

It is here that some formal requirements to use mathematics or science can be included in the question.

Type 6: design strategies

The candidate will be asked to use design strategies for a short design scenario.

The question will be written in a form which requires the student to use a given strategy to carry out design analysis, development or evaluation.

Strategies could include:

- clarifying briefs – turning an open-ended brief into a more specific form
- writing specifications – turning a headline specification into a more detailed form
- attribute analysis – analysing possible product characteristics
- brainstorming – completing a started brainstorm or organizing a random list from a brainstorm to show categories and links
- impact of D&T – interrogating a completed winners and losers chart
- user trip – interpreting user views and opinions.

Example

The candidate will be presented with a series of images showing the reactions of someone using a product. For example, a remote controller – image 1, looking; image 2, holding; image 3, trying out; image 4, changing the batteries, and so on.

The candidate will be told that these photos were taken of someone testing a new remote controller which was designed to … (simple brief). The candidate will be asked to:

- write down what they think the person was asked to do
- how they think this person responded to the product
- write down the reactions of the person testing the product.

Type 7: presenting and interpreting information

The candidate will be asked to make sense of D&T research data.

The question will be written in a form which requires a student to:

- *present* the information clearly
- *interpret* the data and reach conclusions.

Example

The candidate will be given data from some design and technology research which may come from very different sources. It could be about:

- consumer preferences
- the results of testing a material or component
- production figures for different manufacturing methods
- sales figures for different products.

To present

- Draw a graph or chart to show what people of different age groups thought about the old version of something as compared with the new version.
- Think carefully about which would be the most appropriate form of graph or chart to use present the data clearly.

To interpret

- Which age group of consumers has changed its views most about personal stereos?
- Write down which group you think it is and give reasons for your view.

Type 8: interpreting a short Case Study

The candidate will be asked to use *comprehension* skills, design *strategies* and *knowledge* to demonstrate their *understanding* about D&T activity from the world outside school.

The question will be written in a form which requires the student to:

- *find* a piece of *information* from the text
- *explain* something that is described in the text
- *make judgements* about the quality and effects of the design and technology described.
  It is here also that the application of science or mathematics may be built into the question.

Example

The Case Study could present information about the way circuit board design and manufacturing methods have changed over the last 30 years.

The candidate could be asked to:

Find information

- When was the UV process first used for circuit boards?
- How are printed circuit boards made?

Explain

- Explain the advantages and disadvantages of using surface-mounted components for producing circuits.

Make judgements

- Explain why some pressure groups campaign for robotic mass production techniques to be limited.
- Explain why many large companies are investing in developing robotic manufacturing systems which have sight and component recognition capabilities.

This chapter provides a brief summary of the requirements of different Examination Boards and indicates those syllabuses that are supported by Nuffield materials.

City and Guilds of London Institute

City & Guilds

Courses being offered

The following are being offered as both full and short GCSE courses:

Design and Technology (unendorsed – two focus areas)
Design and Technology: Resistant Materials Technology ✓
Design and Technology: Food Technology ✓
Design and Technology: Textile Technology ✓
Design and Technology: Graphic Products ✓
Design and Technology: Electronic Products ✓

A combined course in Design and technology and Business Enterprise will also be offered.

✓ Are supported by Nuffield materials

Coursework requirements

This is in two parts:

- candidates are required to produce an integrated design and make project duration approximately 20 hours for a short course or 40 hours for a full course

- candidates are required to produce a written product evaluation report on an existing product.

Coursework accounts for 60% of the total marks (one third for designing, two thirds for making) and will be moderated by external moderators visiting the centre.

Examination requirements

For the short course candidates are required to take a 1.25 hour examination based on section A of the syllabus.

For the full course candidates are required to take the same 1.25 hours examination as the short course candidates plus a further paper of 1.25 hours based on section B of the syllabus. The examination counts for 40% of the total marks (50% designing, 50% making); there are two tiers for written papers: A*–D and C–G.

Key features

- Allows candidates to specialise in a single materials focus area or work in two focus areas.

- Provides a teacher support guide.

- Links with GNVQ's at Foundation and Intermediate levels.

- Detailed assessment coursework grid with criteria for each GCSE grade.

- External moderator support.

- Specified requirements of design applications in an industrial context.

- Prepares students for the technological world requiring them to design and make products in response to needs and opportunities.

For further information contact:
Subject Officer, 46 Britannia Street, London, WC1X 9RG
Tel: 0171 294 2468 Fax: 0171 294 2400

Midland Examining Group

Courses being offered

The following are being offered as both full and short GCSE courses:

D&T: Resistant Materials Technology✓   D&T: Textile Technology✓

D&T: Graphic Products✓   D&T: Electronic Products✓

D&T: Food Technology✓

The following are being offered as full GCSE courses only:

D&T: Systems and Control Products; D&T: Automotive Engineering.

D&T Engineering is offered as both full and dual award.

✓Are supported by Nuffield materials

Coursework requirements

All coursework has an overall weighting of 60%. For syllabuses offered as both full and short GCSE courses candidates are required to complete a coursework project – a design folder and realisation of a quality product. For the full course this represents 40/60 hours of curriculum time and for the short course 20/30 hours.

For D&T Systems and Control Products candidates are required to complete a coursework project – a design folder and the realisation of a system/control product. For D&T Automotive Engineering candidates are required to complete coursework project – a design folder and the realisation of a system/control product (40%) and practical assignments (20%). For D&T Engineering candidates are required to produce a portfolio selection of work. In addition, dual aware candidates will have to complete a response to an Engineering Design Brief and an Engineering Report.

Examination requirements

All terminal examinations have an overall weighting of 40%. There are two tiers of entry: higher – A* to D (U)   Foundation – C to G

For the syllabuses being offered as both full and short GCSE courses candidates taking a short course take one paper; candidates taking a full course take two papers.

For D&T: Systems and Control Products candidates take two papers – Paper 1: Core; Paper 2: Option. For D&T: Automotive Engineering candidates take one paper. For D&T: Engineering candidates complete a Board set Capability Task (Duration 10 hours); and take one paper for the single award or two papers for the dual award.

Key features

- All coursework internally assessed and standardised, moderation will be by visit.

- Allows candidates to produce a realistic product for coursework.

- New, 'user friendly' coursework assessment scheme.

- Full INSET programme commenced October 1995.

For further information contact:

Subject Officer, Midlands Examining Group, Robins Wood House, Robins Wood Road, Aspley, Nottingham, NG8 3NR Tel: 0115 929 6021 Fax: 0115 929 5261

Different Examination Boards

Northern Examinations and Assessment Board

Courses being offered

The following are being offered as both full and short GCSE courses:

Design and Technology: Resistant Materials ✓
Design and Technology: Graphic Products ✓
Design and Technology: Food Technology ✓
Design and Technology: Textile Technology ✓
Design and Technology: Electronic Products ✓

The following is being offered as full GCSE courses only:

Design and Technology: Systems.
✓ Are supported by Nuffield materials

Coursework requirements

Coursework submission is 60% of the overall assessment (20% designing and 40% making). Candidates are required to complete a major project consisting of a design folder and a practical outcome. The project will be assessed holistically using the two assessment objectives, Designing and Making.

The time to be spent on the project will depend on the material area. The short course requirements are half those for the full course, e.g., Design and Technology: Resistant Materials about 50/25 hours, Design and Technology: Food Technology 25/12 hours.

Examination requirements

Examination counts for 40% of the total marks. All candidates sit a single written paper, set at two tiers, with separate papers for the full and short course.

For the full course Higher level candidates (Grades A*–D) take a written paper of 2.5 hours and Foundation level candidates (Grades C–G) take a 2 hour written paper.

For the short course Higher level candidates (Grades A*–D) take a written paper for 2 hours and Foundation level candidates (Grades C–G) take a 1.5 hour written paper.

Key features

- All syllabuses build on the good practice developed in the current Design and Technology syllabuses.

- Each syllabus may be delivered by an individual teacher.

- A wide range of materials may be used in the Resistant Materials syllabus.

- Common syllabus section based on Key Stage 4 Design and Technology Programme of Study for designing and making.

- Moderation is by inspection, normally by visiting moderators.

- Teachers will be supported by meetings, both before teaching starts and during the course.

For further information contact:

Subject Officer, NEAB, Wheatfield Road, Westerhope, Newcastle-upon-tyne, NE5 5JZ
Tel: 0191 201 0180 Fax: 0191 271 3314

RSA Examinations Board

Courses being offered

The following are being offered as both full and short GCSE courses:

Design and Technology (unendorsed, multi-material, covering Resistant Materials)✓
Design and Technology: Textiles Technology✓
Design and Technology: Food Technology✓
Design and Technology: Graphical Products✓
✓Are supported by Nuffield materials

Coursework requirements

Coursework accounts for 60% of the total marks (one third for designing, two thirds for making) and will be moderated by externally-appointed moderators visiting the centre.

Candidates are required to produce a portfolio of work including a substantial designing and making task. The substantial task should take approximately 20 hours for the short course and approximately 40 hours for the full course.

Examination requirements

Examination counts for 40% of the total marks divided equally between designing and making.

For the short course candidates are required to take a one hour examination based on a scenario set by RSA in advance of the examination which will draw on the knowledge, skills and understanding identified for the GCSE (short course) including the chosen manufacturing material area.

For the full course, in addition to taking the same one hour examination as the short course candidates, candidates will take a further one hour extension paper to show more detailed knowledge and understanding of working with a design specification in the industrial manufacturing material area they have chosen.

Key features

- Allows candidates to specialise in a single material or work in more than one material.

- Provides full teacher support including a support pack and INSET.

- Allows credit towards GNVQ Intermediate Manufacturing Units.

For further information contact:

Subject Officer, RSA Examination Board, Westward Way, Coventry,
West Midlands CV4 8HS Tel: 01203 470033 Fax: 01203 468080

Different Examination Boards

⑦ Southern Examining Group

Courses being offered

Both full and short courses are offered.

The Design and Technology full course syllabus (3400) consists of two parts:

1) a common syllabus section and 2) an area of focus. Candidates choose from one of the following areas of focus:

Electronic Products ✓

Graphic Products ✓

Systems and Control Products

Product Design and Manufacture ✓

Food Technology ✓

Textile Technology ✓

The Design and Technology short course (1400) consists of the common syllabus section only without the areas of focus.

✓Are supported by Nuffield materials

Coursework requirements

Coursework submission is 60% of the overall assessment (40% for designing skills, 60% for making skills). Candidates are required to submit an assignment integrating designing and making supported by additional tasks, or alternatively two integrated assignments. Coursework submission may be achieved through the common syllabus content and one area of focus. Moderation will be by area moderation meetings under the direction of a SEG moderator.

Examination requirements

The written papers of the examination are 40% of the overall assessment (40% for designing and 60% for making).

For the full course candidates are required to take a written paper of 1.5 hours on the common syllabus section and a written paper of 1 hour on their chosen area of focus.

For the short course candidates are required to take a written paper of 1.5 hours on the common syllabus section.

Key features

- Common syllabus section based on Key Stage 4 Programme of Study for Design and Technology.

- Builds upon the Key Stage 3 Programme of Study for Design and Technology.

- Allows centres a flexible approach to the subject.

- Provides a comprehensive teacher support package, including printed exemplar materials, regional support meetings and experienced staff for dealing with queries.

For further information contact:

Subject Officer, Southern Examining Group, Staghill House, Guildford, Surrey, GU2 5XJ
Tel: 01483 506506 Fax: 01483 300152

Edexcel Foundation

The following are being offered as both full and short GCSE courses:

Design and Technology: Product Design✓

Design and Technology: Graphic Products✓

Design and Technology: Electronic Products✓

Design and Technology: Food Technology✓

Design and Technology: Textile Technology✓

The following combined course is being offered:

Design and Technology: Product Design and Business.

✓Are supported by Nuffield materials

Coursework requirements

Coursework accounts for 60% of the total marks for both full and short courses.

For the full course, candidates will have to produce one major Capability Task (40%) taking approximately 30 hours and an assignment (20%) taking approximately 10 hours.

For the short course: candidates will have to produce one major Capability Task (40%) taking approximately 15 hours and an assignment (20%) taking approximately 5 hours.

Themes for the tasks will be chosen by candidates and approved by teachers in accordance with their chosen focus area and lines of interest. Edexcel will provide exemplar material to guide teachers in selecting and setting tasks.

Examination requirements

The written papers of the examination are 40% of the overall assessment.

The full course examination lasts 2.5 hours.

The short course examination lasts 1.5 hours.

Key features

- Each syllabus has a single focus area which allows candidates to develop their skills of designing and making and their knowledge and understanding in a field of special interest to them.

- The skills, knowledge and understanding of this syllabus may be realised in a variety of contexts, according to the resources available and the interests of teacher and candidates.

- The Council will provide teacher support and guidance for the coursework and for the syllabus.

For further information contact

Subject Officer, Edexcel Foundation, Stewart House, 32 Russell Square, London, WC1B 5DN

Tel: 0171 331 4000 Fax: 0171 753 4558

⑦ Welsh Joint Education Committee

Courses being offered

Design and Technology is being offered as full, combined and short GCSE courses in the five combined syllabuses. Design and Technology may be taken with either Art, Business Studies, Catering, Electronics or Information Technology.

All courses may be delivered through one or more of the following six focus areas:

Control   Product Design✓
Food✓   Resistant Materials✓
Graphic Media✓   Textiles✓.

✓Are supported by Nuffield materials

Coursework requirements

Coursework submission is 60% of the overall assessment and there is a 40 : 60 weighting between designing and making.

For a full course candidates are required to complete a single substantial design and make project, which may be based on one or more of the focus areas.

For a short course candidates are required to complete a single substantial design and make project, which may be based on one or more of the focus areas but the depth of study and time commitment of the project is reduced compared to the full course.

Project work will be assessed by the centre and a sample moderated by a visiting examiner.

Examination requirements and weightings

The written papers of the examination are 40% of the overall assessment. For the full course there will be a terminal examination consisting of two papers, totalling 2.5 hours duration:

Paper 1 is common to all focus areas;

Paper 2 is specific to a single focus area – candidates select one from six.

Candidates will be required to demonstrate designing skills and an understanding of making skills applicable to at least one of the focus areas.

For short and combined courses candidates sit only Paper 1.

Key features

- Develops candidates' competence to address a wide variety of design situations by drawing upon a broad base of knowledge and skills.

- The syllabus provides the opportunity for a number of existing curriculum areas to make a contribution to the examination.

- The syllabus is sufficiently broad, balanced and relevant to interest all candidates.

For further information contact:

Subject Officer, Welsh Joint Education Committee, 245 Western Avenue, Cardiff Wales, CF5 2YX Tel: 01222 265000 Fax: 01222 575994

Resource Task Summary Tables ⑧

Task number and title	Learning	Type of task	Links with other subjects	Time	Demand	Capability Tasks supported
SRT 1 Identifying needs and likes	To identify needs and likes.	Recap		Part 1: 40 minutes Part 2: 40 minutes	*	Pet protection, Plant protection, Automatic weighing machine, Environment monitoring, Light and sound, Radical radios
SRT 2 Questionnaires	To use information collected in a survey. To use a database to handle the information.	New	IT	120 minutes	***	Troubled travels, Lock it up, Safe and sound, Radio control toys
SRT 3 Design briefs and specifications	To write design briefs in response to needs, wants and likes. To write a specification from a design brief.	Extension		Part 1: 40 minutes Part 2: 40 minutes	**	Can be used with any Capability Task
SRT 4 Brainstorming	To apply two sorts of brainstorming.	Extension		Part 1: 40 minutes Part 2: 40 minutes	**	Pet protection, Plant protection, Light and sound
SRT 5 Attribute analysis	To extend your understanding of how to use attribute analysis to think up different ideas for a product.	Extension		45 minutes	**	Troubled travels
SRT 6 Evaluating	To extend your understanding of how to evaluate a design by thinking how it affects people, whether it performs as expected, and is appropriate.	Extension		Part 1: 40 minutes Part 2: 40 minutes Part 3: 40 minutes Part 4: 40 minutes	**	Can be used with any Capability Task
SRT 7 Systems and control	To use systems thinking.	Extension		Part 1: 40 minutes Part 2: 40 minutes	**	Can be used with any Capability Task

Demand ✳ = low in demand   ✳✳ = moderately demanding   ✳✳✳ = very demanding

Task number and title	Learning	Type of task	Links with other subjects	Time	Demand	Capability Tasks supported
CRT 1 Communicating ideas to the client	How to use shading and colour to communicate the appearance of a product to a client.	Recap		40 minutes	**	Light and sound, Display system, Radio control toys
CRT 2 Communicating ideas to the maker 1: construction and assembly	How to produce orthographic drawings to enable the casing of an electronic product to be made.	Extension		120 minutes	***	Troubled travels, Lock it up, Warehousing robot
CRT 3 Communicating ideas to the maker 2: circuit diagrams to practical layouts	How to construct a practical layout from a circuit diagram.	New		80 minutes	**	Troubled travels, Lock it up, Warehousing robot
CRT 4 Communicating to the user	How to use graphical skills to produce a user guide.	Extension	IT	180 minutes	**	Pet protection, Plant protection, Environment monitoring, Light and sound, Radical radios
ECRT 1 Controlling a simple buggy	To construct an electrical control circuit from a circuit diagram.	Recap	Science	120 minutes	*	Automatic weighing machine, Display system, Warehousing robot, Mars Lander
ECRT 2 Choosing batteries	To use meters to measure voltage and current in a circuit. To match the power requirements of a circuit to a power source.	New	Science	Part 1: 20 minutes Part 2: 40 minutes	***	Automatic weighing machine, Warehousing robot
SBRT 1 Sensing and processing with transistors	To use a transistor in simple sensing circuits by means of systems boards.	Recap and Extension	Science	Part 1: 20 minutes Part 2: 40 minutes	**	Pet protection, Automatic weighing machine, Environment monitoring, Safe and sound, Display system, Warehousing robot, Mars Lander
SBRT 2 Using a comparator	To use a comparator for analogue to digital signal conversion by means of systems boards.	New		Part 1: 20 minutes Part 2: 20 minutes Part 3: 20 minutes	***	Plant protection, Automatic weighing machine, Environment monitoring, Warehousing robot, Mars Lander
SBRT 3 Introducing timing into circuits	To design timing circuits with a desired time delay.	New		Part 1: 30 minutes Part 2: 30 minutes	**	Light and sound, Troubled travels, Radio control toys, Mars Lander
SBRT 4 Combining signals	To combine digital and analogue signals by means of systems boards.	New	Maths	Part 1: 45 minutes Part 2: 45 minutes	**	Automatic weighing machine, Light and sound, Mars Lander
SBRT 5 Circuits that count	To use counting circuits by means of systems boards.	New	Maths	Part 1: 60 minutes Part 2: 30 minutes	***	Lock it up, Mars Lander

Resource Task Summary Tables

Task number and title	Learning	Type of task	Links with other subjects	Time	Demand	Capability Tasks link
IBRT 1 Investigating transistor circuits	To design, model and evaluate transistor circuits.	Recap and Extension	Science	Part 1: 60 minutes Part 2: 60 minutes	*	Pet protection, Automatic weighing machine, Environment monitoring, Safe and sound, Display system, Warehousing robot, Mars Lander
IBRT 2 Investigating a comparator	To know how comparator circuits operate.	New		60 minutes	***	Plant protection, Automatic weighing machine, Environment monitoring, Warehousing robot, Mars Lander
IBRT 3 Designing timing circuits	How 555 timer ICs can be configured to provide a range of timing circuits.	New		Part 1: 20 minutes Part 2: 20 minutes Part 3: 20 minutes	**	Light and sound, Troubled travels, Mars Lander
IBRT 4 Designing logic circuits	How to use digital gates to design both combinational and sequential logic circuits.	New	Maths	Part 1: 60 minutes Part 2: 30 minutes	**	Automatic weighing machine, Light and sound, Mars Lander
IBRT 5 Investigating counting	To design and model digital counting systems.	New	Maths	Part 1: 20 minutes Part 2: 20 minutes Part 3: 20 minutes	***	Lock it up, Mars Lander
MfRT 1 Making circuit layouts using copper tape	How to make a circuit layout using self-adhesive copper tape.	New	IT	70 minutes	*	Safe and sound
MfRT 2 Making printed circuit boards	How to make a printed circuit board and build up a circuit on it. The board will be produced by using photo-sensitive board.	New	IT	120 minutes	**	Environment monitoring, Lock it up, Safe and sound
MfRT 3 Assembling an electromechanical system	To assemble simple electrical and mechanical systems from given components.	Extension	Science	90 minutes	**	Automatic weighing machine, Display system, Warehousing robot, Radio control toys, Mars Lander
MfRT 4 Producing enclosures	To produce a variety of enclosures for electronic products.	Extenstion		90 minutes	**	Pet protection, Plant protection, Environment monitoring, Light and sound, Troubled travels. Radical radios

Task number and title	Learning	Type of task	Links with other subjects	Time	Demand	Capability Tasks link
CCRT 1 Component sorting	To recognise different kinds of component. To read the values or types of a component.	Recap	Science Maths	Part 1: 30 minutes Part 2: 30 minutes	*	Pet protection, Lock it up, Safe and sound
CCRT 2 Resistor equations	To use Ohm's Law. To use the power equation. To calculate the values of resistors in series or parallel.	Recap and Extension	Science Maths	Part 1: 20 minutes Part 2: 20 minutes Part 3: 20 minutes	**	Can be used with any Capability Task
CCRT 3 Working with transistors and op-amps	To control voltage with a potential divider. To use transistor gain when designing circuits. To design op-amp circuits with a desired gain.	New	Science Maths	Part 1: 20 minutes Part 2: 20 minutes Part 3: 20 minutes	***	Plant protection, Warehousing robot
CCRT 4 Capacitor equations	To control time delays with an RC network. To calculate the values of capacitors in series or parallel.	New	Science Maths	Part 1: 40 minutes Part 2: 20 minutes	***	Light and sound, Troubled travels
CTRT 1 Making and testing a radio (based on the TEP radio)	How to make and test a simple radio	New	Science	Part 1: 80 minutes Part 2: 10 minutes Part 3: 10 minutes Part 4: 10 minutes Part 5: 10 minutes	**	Radical radios, Mars Lander
PICRT 1 Using microcontrollers	To know when the use of programmable ics might be appropriate. To appreciate the capabilities and limitations of programmable ICs.	New	IT	60 minutes	**	Display system, Mars Lander
PICRT 2 Comparing simple programmable and hard-wired systems	To use a programming environment to create a simple control system. To compare a programmable control system with a hard-wired system.	New	IT	Part 1: 60 minutes Part 2: 60 minutes	***	Display system, Mars Lander
PICRT 3 Developing sophisticated systems	To use a programming environment to create a complex control system. To transfer a program to a programmable IC and test this. To compare a programmable control system with a hard-wired system.	New	IT	Part 1: 90 minutes Part 2: 90 minutes	***	Display system, Mars Lander
PART 1 Looking at a single product	To extend your understanding of how to investigate products.	Recap and Extension	Geography	80 minutes	**	Can be used with any Capability Task
PART 2 Looking at a collection of products	To extend your understanding of how to investigate products.	Recap and Extension	IT	40 minutes	**	Can be used with any Capability Task
HSRT 1 Ensuring safety in an unfamiliar situation	To revise and extend your understanding of how to be safe, and ensure the safety of others.	Recap and Extension		45 minutes	*	Can be used with any Capability Task

Part 2

Capability Tasks for 14–16 year-olds

Capability Task Summary Tables

Line of interest	Task title	Nature of product	Useful Resource Tasks	Useful Case Studies In the Student's Book	Useful other references
Sensing devices	Pet protection	A sensing device which will operate an alarm signal. The output signal could be audible or visual and could be operated directly by the output of the circuit or through a relay. A more able student will produce a more complex output signal such as flashing lights, or a second output in a remote location.	SRT 1 Identifying needs and likes CRT 4 Communicating to the user CCRT 1 Component sorting SBRT 1 Sensing and processing with transistors IBRT 1 Investigating transistor circuits SRT 4 Brainstorming MfRT 4 Producing enclosures	Helping to keep air breathable Sensing devices – IPAS joist/wiring detector	Design guide – sensing devices page 117 Making your own enclosure page 180
Sensing devices	Plant protection	A sensing circuit based on a 741 op amp combined with probes to sense the moisture content of the soil of a pot plant. The state of the soil – too wet, too dry or just right might be shown visually by coloured LEDs or audibly by different sounding buzzers. The device should be placed in a suitable container which is large enough to contain the two batteries needed for the op amp supply and an ON/OFF switch.	SRT 1 Identifying needs and likes SBRT 2 Using a comparator IBRT 2 Investigating a comparator CCRT 3 Working with transistors and op-amps CRT 4 Communicating to the user SRT 4 Brainstorming MfRT 4 Producing enclosures	Helping to keep air breathable Sensing devices – joist/wiring detector	Design guide – sensing devices page 117 Making your own enclosure page 180
Measuring devices	Automatic weighing machine	A small battery powered weighing machine which can accurately and reliably weigh a small mass of about 250 grams. It should display the weight by some electronic means either in digital or analogue form. Considerable extension to a basic concept exists so that automatic batch weighing could be developed by the more able students or students working in a group.	SRT 1 Identifying needs and likes SBRT 1 Sensing and processing with transistors SBRT 2 Using a comparator SBRT 4 Circuits that count IBRT 1 Investigating transistor circuits IBRT 2 Investigating a comparator IBRT 5 Investigating counting MfRT 3 Assembling an electromechanical system ECRT 1 Controlling a simple buggy ECRT 2 Choosing batteries	Helping to keep air breathable Measuring devices – exercise cycle	Design guide – measuring devices page 118 Basic electrics page 125 Basic mechanics page 129

Line of interest	Task title	Nature of product	Useful Resource Tasks	Useful Case Studies in the Student's Book	Useful other references
Measuring devices	Environment monitoring	A measuring device which will provide information about an environmental condition. The output signal may be read from a ready made meter or on a purpose built display. A more able student will calibrate the read out.	SRT 1 Identifying needs and likes SRT 2 Questionnaires SBRT 1 Sensing and processing with transistors SBRT 2 Using a comparator IBRT 1 Investigating transistor circuits IBRT 2 Investigating a comparator CRT 4 Communicating to the user MfRT 2 Making printed circuit boards MfRT 4 Producing enclosures	Helping to keep air breathable Measuring devices – exercise cycle	Design guide – measuring instruments page 118 Making your own enclosure page 180
Electronic novelties	Light and sound	There is a wide variety of possible products, for example: • special effects sound makers; • door chimes; • simple musical instrument; • seasonal light-up displays; • light-up jewellery. For some of these dedicated ICs are available; others can be developed from standard components. Whatever product is developed, it is important that the item produced is considered from both the aesthetic and technical viewpoints.	SRT 1 Identifying needs and wants SRT 4 Brainstorming SBRT 3 Introducing timing into circuits SBRT 5 Circuits that count IBRT 3 Designing timing circuits IBRT 5 Investigating counting CRT 1 Communicating ideas to the client CRT 4 Communicating to the user CCRT 4 Capacitor equations MfRT 4 Producing enclosures	Electronic novelties – 'soft' noise making toys	Design guide – electronic novelties page 119 Making your own enclosure page 180
Electronic novelties	Troubled travels	In its simplest form, the product will consist of a maze type challenge to be completed against the monostable time delay. This offers a variety of thermoplastic case design opportunities allied to developing an understanding of the timer circuit. Scope for electronic development includes addition of: • an astable circuit for flashing lights or imaginative sounds; • a variety of clock and counter opportunities for digital time delay; • logic opportunities, for example, five balls in their sequentially correct maze positions sets output.	SRT 2 Questionnaires SRT 5 Attribute analysis SBRT 3 Introducing timing into circuits IBRT 3 Designing timing circuits CRT 2 Communicating ideas to the maker 1 CRT 3 Communicating ideas to the maker 2 CCRT4 Capacitor equations MfRT 4 Producing enclosures	Electronic novelties – 'soft' noise making toys	Design guide – electronic novelties page 119 Making your own enclosure page 180

Capability Task Summary Tables

Line of interest	Task title	Nature of product	Useful Resource Tasks	Useful Case Studies In the Student's Book	Useful other references
Security devices	Lock it up	An electronic lock operated by the output of a set of logic gates; input to the gates by push switches. When the final output is high a solenoid operates, opening a lock. Options include: • correct switches in any sequence operate lock; • dummy switches which if pressed prevent unlocking; • switches must be pushed in a particular sequence; • dummy switches not connected make the sequence harder to guess; • using a key pad; • a lock out facility to prevent the door from opening if any of the dummy switches are pressed; • an alarm to warn if any incorrect switches are pressed; • an automatic reset which operates when the door is opened and closed.	SRT 2 Questionnaires CRT 2 Communicating ideas to the maker 1 CRT 3 Communicating ideas to the maker 2 CCRT 1 Component sorting SBRT 4 Combining signals IBRT 1 Designing logic circuits MfRT 2 Making printed circuit boards	Security devices – intruder alarms for cars	Design guide – security devices page 120 Making your own enclosure page 180
Security devices	Safe and sound	A sensing device for a school or sports bag which will operate an alarm signal if the bag is tampered with. The output signal should stay on once operated. A more able student might develop a range of possible output signals.	SRT 2 Questionnaires CRT 4 Communicating to the user CCRT 1 Component sorting SBRT 1 Sensing and processing with transistors IBRT 1 Investigating transistor circuits MfRT 1 Making circuit layouts using copper tape MfRT 2 Making printed circuit boards	Security devices – intruder alarms for cars	Design guide – security devices page 120 Making your own enclosure page 180

Line of interest	Task title	Nature of product	Useful Resource Tasks	Useful Case Studies in the Student's Book	Useful other references
Control systems	Display system	A completely automated display of an area of industrial or commercial activity. This could be a large and complex task suitable for a team of students in which each student is responsible for a particular feature of the display and the team as a whole is responsible for integrating each feature into the overall display. There is the opportunity of working closely with a local industry and producing a display that is the centrepiece of their main reception area. The control functions within the display will lend themselves to the use of programmable logic controller ICs.	PICRT 1 Using micro controllers PICRT 2 Comparing simple programmable and hard-wired systems PICRT 3 Developing sophisticated systems SBRT 1 Sensing and processing with transistors IBRT 1 Investigating transistor circuits CRT 1 Communicating ideas to the client CRT 2 Communicating ideas to the maker 1 CRT 3 Communicating ideas to the maker 2 MfRT 3 Assembling an electromechanical system ECRT 1 Controlling a simple buggy	Communicating devices – bus arrival times system, the countdown service	Design guide – control systems page 121 Basic electrics page 125 Basic mechanics page 129 Programmable ICs page 168
Control systems	Ware-housing robot	A small battery powered motorized robot 'buggy' which will automatically follow a track marked on a flat surface or a 'buried' current carrying wire. Depending on what type of sensing, electronics, drive system and steering ideas are used, there exists considerable scope for variation and development from the basic device.	SBRT 1 Sensing and processing with transistors SBRT 2 Using a comparator IBRT 1 Investigating transistor circuits IBRT 2 Investigating a comparator CCRT 3 Working with transistors and op amps CRT 2 Communicating ideas to the maker 1 CRT 3 Communicating ideas to the maker 2 MfRT 3 Assembling an electromechanical system ECRT 1 Controlling a simple buggy ECRT 2 Choosing batteries	Communicating devices – bus arrival times system, the countdown service	Design guide – control systems page 121 Basic electrics page 125 Basic mechanics page 129
Communicating devices	Radical radios	A radio that is suited for use in a particular situation. A given radio circuit, such as the TEP FM radio, can be used as the basic circuit. Students can adjust for optimum performance and experiment with different speakers and headsets. The more able student may be encouraged to calibrate the reception dial and develop sensitive tuning mechanisms.	SRT 1 Identifying needs and likes SRT 5 Attribute analysis CRT 1 Communicating ideas to the client MfRT 4 Producing enclosures CRT 4 Communicating to the user CTRT 1 Making and testing a radio (based on the TEP radio)	Communicating devices – clockwork radio A radio revolution	Design guide – communicating page 122 Using radio technology page 165

Capability Task Summary Tables

© The Nuffield Foundation, 1997

Line of interest	Task title	Nature of product	Useful Resource Tasks	Useful Case Studies in the Student's Book	Useful other references
Communicating devices	Radio control toys	A radio-control model that is suitable for a particular user. A less able student might disassemble an existing toy and build the receiver, transmitter and servos into a model of their own design. A more able student might build the circuitry from existing plans.	SRT 2 Questionnaires SRT 4 Brainstorming SBRT 3 Introducing timing into circuits PART 1 Looking at a single product (This can be adapted to look specifically at simple radio control models) MfRT 3 Assembling an electromechanical system CRT 1 Communicating ideas to the client	Communicating devices – bus arrival times system, the countdown service	Design guide – communicating page 122 Using radio technology page 165
Multiple line products	Mars Lander	A prototype small scale buggy that can survive a parachute landing, move around its surroundings collecting data which it transmits to a remote reception centre.	ECRT 1 Controlling a simple buggy SBRT 1 Sensing and processing with transistors SBRT 2 Using a comparator SBRT 3 Introducing timing into circuits SBRT 4 Combining signals SBRT 5 Circuits that count IBRT 1 Investigating transistor circuits IBRT 2 Investigating a comparator IBRT 3 Designing timing circuits IBRT 4 Designing logic circuits IBRT 5 Investigating counting MfRT 3 Assembling an electromechanical system CTRT 1 Making and testing a radio (based on the TEP radio) PICRT 1 Using micro controllers PICTR 2 Comparing simple programmable and hard-wired systems PICRT 3 Developing sophisticated systems	Communicating devices – bus arrival times system, the countdown service Helping to keep air breathable	Basic electrics page 125 Basic mechanics page 129 Programmable ICs page 168

Pet protection ①

The task

To design and construct an electronic system which will warn an owner when changes in environmental conditions (such as temperature, humidity, light) will affect the well-being of a pet or small farm animal.

Task setting

Domestic pets and small farm animals often need some sort of protection from environmental changes such as extremes of temperature, variations in humidity, food or water running low, etc. The task is to identify an environmental condition which would affect a particular mammal, reptile, bird or fish, and then to design and make a sensing device which will show when that condition reaches a level that could cause harm to the animal. The product is to be designed for small-batch production and, depending on its intended use, would be sold by a pet shop or by suppliers of equipment for farmers and would be bought by the owners of pets or small animals.

The aims of the task

- to enable students to identify the environmental needs of an animal and how changes in environmental conditions will affect the animal
- to enable students to identify which type of sensing device and output device would be most appropriate for the task
- to enable students to understand how a signal from a sensing device can be amplified and can operate an output device
- to enable students to develop skills in designing and making a shell for the circuit and also a user guide.

Values

technical
Students should understand the environmental factor involved and the most appropriate way in which changes can be sensed.

economic
Students should appreciate the production methods which are appropriate for small-batch production.

aesthetic
Students should design a case for the product which is appropriate to the purpose of the device and the place where it will be used.

moral
Students should consider the issues involved in keeping animals in confined spaces.

social
Students should consider issues related to keeping animals to provide company for those who live alone.

environmental
Students should consider the effect of keeping animals on the domestic environment.

Nature of the product

A sensing device which will operate an alarm signal. The output signal could be audible or visual and could be operated directly by the output of the circuit or through a relay. A more able candidate will produce a more complex output signal, such as flashing lights, or a second output in a remote location.

Technical knowledge and understanding

- knowledge of suitable sensors
- knowledge of suitable processing circuits
- knowledge of suitable output devices
- knowledge of enclosure production techniques.

Specialist tools, materials and equipment

- a range of suitable sensors – thermistors, light-dependent resistors, water probes
- a range of suitable processors – BFY51 and BC108 transistors
- a range of suitable output devices – LEDs, lamps, buzzers
- access to prototype boards or systems kits for modelling, investigating and developing possible circuits is useful
- PCB production facilities
  Possible suppliers:
  Maplin MPS on 01702 554000
  Rapid Electronics on 01206 751166
- vacuum forming facilities.

© The Nuffield Foundation, 1997

Cross-curricular links

maths
- measurements of operating and quiescent current drain can be used to calculate likely battery life.

science
- relevant concepts concerning the environmental factors which affect small animals.

art
- observational drawings of small animals and pets can be used to inform the overall style and decoration of the enclosure.

IT
- CAD software can be used to design the case and to produce the PCB layout.

economic and industrial understanding
- looking at the cost of similar existing products and relating this to material component and manufacturing costs.

Useful Resource Tasks

To enable students to identify the environmental needs of an animal and how changes in conditions will affect the animal:
- SRT 1 *Identifying needs and likes*.

To enable students to develop skills needed to produce a user guide:
- CRT 4 *Communicating to the user*.

To enable students to identify which type of sensing device and output device would be most appropriate for the task:
- CCRT 1 *Component sorting*
- SBRT 1 *Sensing and processing with transistors*
- IBRT 1 *Investigating transistor circuits*.

To enable students to develop skills in designing and making an enclosure for the circuit:
SRT 4 *Brainstorming*
MfRT 4 *Producing enclosures*.

Useful Case Studies

To enable students to understand how a signal from a sensing device can be amplified and can operate an output device:
- Helping to keep air breathable
- Sensing devices – joist/wiring detector.

Design brief

To design and make a sensing device which will activate an alarm when one or more of the environmental conditions necessary for a small mammal, bird, fish or reptile to survive comfortably are outside of a desired limit. The device will be bought by the owner of the creature involved and may be used in a domestic situation or in small-scale production, such as on a farm. It will be sold in a pet shop or by a company which supplies farm equipment.

Preliminary specification

What the product should do:
- sense a change in environmental conditions
- work accurately within a defined variation in the environmental condition
- provide a suitable output signal.

What the product should look like:
- suit the purpose of the device
- suit the location in which the product will be used.

Other features:
- powered from a battery
- have an ON/OFF switch
- have facilities to replace the battery
- be suitable for small-batch production
- cost no more than £9.50, including the cost of the case.

Design sketches

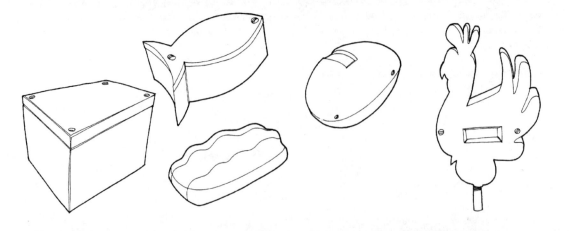

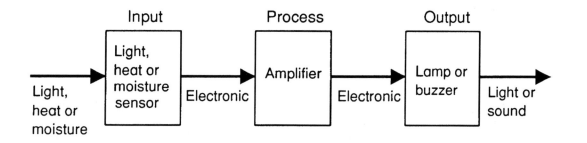

Input — Light, heat or moisture sensor
Process — Amplifier
Output — Lamp or buzzer

Light, heat or moisture → Electronic → Electronic → Light or sound

Information for making

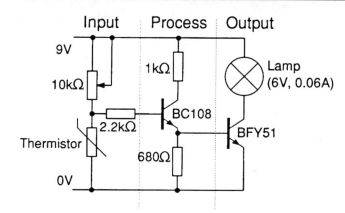

Likely solution

A Darlington pair circuit operated by a suitable sensor, such as a thermistor, LDR, moisture, etc., and operating a suitable output device such as an LED, buzzer, etc.

A basic circuit for a low-temperature alarm system

The lamp will come on when the temperature drops to a level which will cause harm to an animal.

Circuit modification

How would you change the output device to provide an audible alarm of the low temperature?

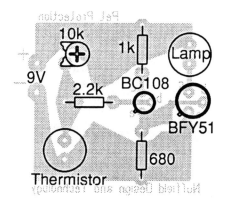
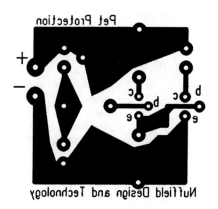

A basic enclosure

This is made from a bought box with a spray paint finish. The lid is fixed with four self-tapping screws into corner blocks.

Enclosure modification

How would you customize a case to reflect your purpose and conditions of use?

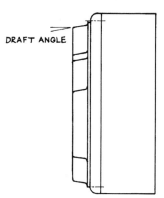
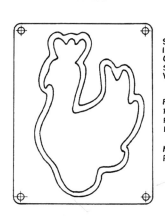
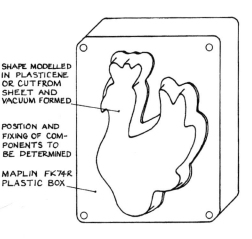

DRAFT ANGLE

SHAPE MODELLED IN PLASTICENE OR CUT FROM SHEET AND VACUUM FORMED

POSITION AND FIXING OF COMPONENTS TO BE DETERMINED

MAPLIN FK74R PLASTIC BOX

END ELEVATION   FRONT ELEVATION   OBLIQUE VIEW

FIRST ANGLE ORTHOGRAPHIC PROJECTION

© The Nuffield Foundation, 1997

② Plant protection

A Capability Task for electronics
Line of interest – sensing devices

The task

To design and construct an electronic system which will inform an owner of pot plants when the soil is too dry or too moist.

Task setting

Some plants grown indoors, or in a greenhouse, need careful watering. Too much water or too little water can damage them. The task is to identify a need for such a warning system and then to design and make a sensing device which can be used to test the moisture content of the soil. The product should be suitable for small-batch production and would be sold in garden centres.

The aims of the task

- to enable students to identify the needs of people who keep plants and flowers
- to enable students to identify which type of sensing device and output device would be most appropriate for the task
- to enable students to understand and use an operational amplifier as a processing device
- to enable students to develop skills in designing and making a shell for the circuit and also a user guide.

Values

technical

Students should understand the moisture requirements involved and the most appropriate way in which changes can be sensed.

economic

Students should appreciate the methods which are appropriate for small-batch production.

aesthetic

tudents should design a case for the product which is appropriate to the purpose of the device and the place where it will be used.

moral

Students should consider the use of electronic methods to replace human activity.

social

Students should consider the act of keeping plants as a hobby which can be shared with others.

environmental

Students should consider the ways in which plants can be used to enhance a domestic or work environment.

Nature of the product

What is required is a sensing circuit based on a 741 op-amp combined with probes to sense the moisture content of the soil of a pot plant. The state of the soil – too wet, too dry or just right (might be shown visually by coloured LEDs or audibly by different-sounding buzzers. The device should be placed in a suitable container which is large enough to contain the two batteries needed for the op-amp supply and an ON/OFF switch.

Technical knowledge and understanding

- knowledge of operational amplifiers
- knowledge of sensors for detecting the low conductivity of water
- knowledge of enclosure production techniques.

Specialist tools, materials and equipment

- 741 op-amp
- 8 pin DIL IC holder
- access to prototype boards or systems kits for modelling, investigating and developing possible circuits is useful
- PCB production facilities
- conductive, corrosion-resistant materials for making moisture probes

Possible suppliers:
Maplin MPS on 01702 554000
Rapid Electronics on 01206 751166
- vacuum forming facilities.

Cross-curricular links

maths

- measurements of operating and quiescent current drain can be used to calculate likely battery life.

science

- relevant concepts concerning the environmental factors affecting plants.

art

- observational drawings of plants and flowers can be used to inform the overall style and decoration of the enclosure.

IT

- CAD software can be used to design the case and to produce the PCB layout.

economic and industrial understanding

- looking at the cost of similar existing products and relating this to material component and manufacturing costs.

Useful Resource Tasks

To enable students to identify the needs of people who keep plants and flowers:
- SRT 1 *Identifying needs and likes.*

To enable students to understand and use an operational amplifier as a processing device:
- SBRT 2 *Using a comparator*
- IBRT 2 *Investigating a comparator*
- CCRT 3 *Working with transistors and op amps.*

To enable students to develop skills needed to produce a user guide:
- CRT 4 *Communicating to the user.*

To enable students to develop skills in designing and making an enclosure for the circuit:
- SRT 4 *Brainstorming*
- MfRT 4 *Producing enclosures.*

Useful Case Studies

To enable students to understand how a signal from a sensing device can be amplified and can operate an output device:
- Helping to keep air breathable
- Sensing devices – joist/wiring detector.

Design brief

Design and make a sensing device which will monitor the moisture content of the soil of a pot plant and which will give a visual indication of when the soil is too dry, at the correct moisture level or too wet.

Preliminary specification

What the product should do:
- sense a change in moisture content of soil
- work accurately within a defined variation in the environmental condition
- provide a suitable output signal through the use of different-coloured LEDs.

What the product should look like:
- suit the purpose of the device
- suit the location in which the product will be used.

Other features:
- powered from a battery
- have an ON/OFF switch
- have facilities to replace the battery
- be suitable for small-batch production
- cost no more than £9.50, including the cost of the case.

Design sketches

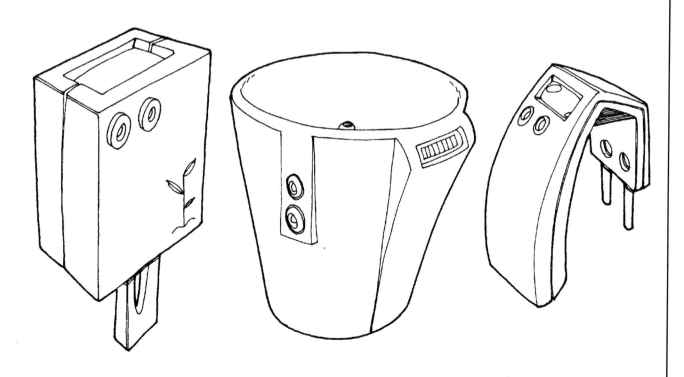

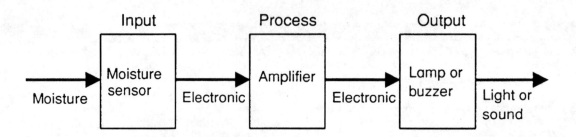

Information for making

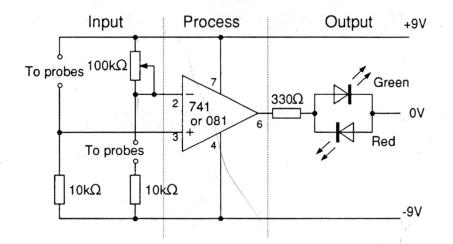

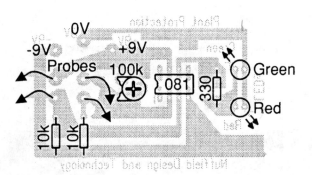

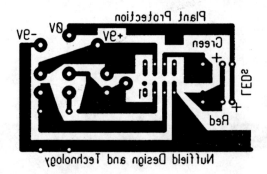

Likely solution
A 741 op-amp circuit using two sets of probes and having two different-coloured LEDs as outputs.

A basic moisture monitoring system
The red LED will come on if there is too little moisture and the green LED will come on if there is too much.

Circuit modification
How would you change the output device to provide an audible indication of each condition?

A basic enclosure
This is made from a bought box with a spray paint finish. The lid is fixed with four self-tapping screws into corner blocks with two sets of moisture-sensing probes attached to the op amp by coiled wire. (Note that this is similar to the enclosure used in Pet Protection, page 49.)

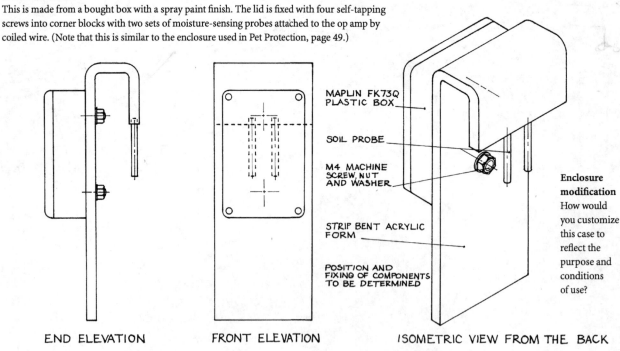

MAPLIN FK73Q PLASTIC BOX
SOIL PROBE
M4 MACHINE SCREW, NUT AND WASHER
STRIP BENT ACRYLIC FORM
POSITION AND FIXING OF COMPONENTS TO BE DETERMINED

Enclosure modification
How would you customize this case to reflect the purpose and conditions of use?

END ELEVATION   FRONT ELEVATION   ISOMETRIC VIEW FROM THE BACK

FIRST ANGLE ORTHOGRAPHIC PROJECTION

Automatic weighing machine ③

The task

To design and make an electronic weighing machine to weigh small masses up to 250 g.

Task setting

In many industries, factories, offices, laboratories or medical and domestic situations a wide variety of goods, equipment and materials need to be weighed, ranging from minute amounts of pharmaceutical chemicals to ocean-going ships. In addition, in packaging plants precise amounts of materials often need to be weighed repeatedly prior to being put into various types of containers. The design should consider the nature of the product to be weighed (such as powder, liquid, solid, size, shape, whether for consumption or otherwise, and so on). Also to be considered is the concept of weight as distinct from mass, and the various principles involved in the ways in which weight may be sensed, bearing in mind that weight is a measure of the force of gravity exerted on an object.

The aims of the task

- to reinforce the technique of electronic design through a systems approach
- to consider and investigate aspects of user interfaces
- to encourage consideration of the accuracy of measurement and factors which affect it
- to reinforce the concept of feedback
- to encourage investigations into the task to develop a better understanding of the problems involved
- to investigate various types of sensing devices and circuits
- to appreciate the factors involved in interfacing electronics to mechanical devices
- to develop a better appreciation of the scientific principles involved
- to develop communication skills
- to develop high quality electronic and mechanical making skills.

Values

technical

Students should investigate a variety of methods of measuring the force of gravity on an object. These should include deflections of various types of springs, and the comparison of forces against those of standard masses.

They should also investigate the relative merits of many ways of electronically sensing the deflection of spring systems and how this may be displayed, possibly remote from where the measurement is made. Accuracy, sensitivity, repeatability and reliability could also be considered as could vibration and the need for damping.

economic

Students should consider the relative costs and benefits or otherwise of automatic weighing systems against those requiring manual operators. They could also investigate the economic needs for weighing and the importance of accuracy and repeatability in batch weighing with regard to the reduction of waste and fairness in distribution.

aesthetic

Students should consider whether or not aesthetics are important in the design of functional machines of this type, considering the use to which the device will be put and who will use it and where. In this instance, four radically different environments could be a domestic kitchen, a steel scrapyard, an ultra-sterile pharmaceutical laboratory and a post-office sorting room. The importance of the user interface should not be overlooked in these contexts.

moral

Students might consider the implications of the need for an internationally accepted standard mass against which all other weights and masses are ultimately compared. They may also consider the role of the Trading and Standards office.

social

Students might consider how automatic weighing systems have affected how we shop, especially in supermarkets and other self-service outlets.

environmental

Students should consider the total energy requirements for the production and use of an automated system. Also to be considered are the repair and maintenance requirements, the expected life of the product and to what extent it could be recycled at the end of its life.

Nature of the product

This is a small, battery-powered weighing machine which can accurately and reliably weigh a small mass of about 250 g. It should display the weight by some electronic means, either in digital or analogue form. Considerable extension to a basic concept exists so that automatic batch weighing could be developed by a more able student or by students working in a group.

Technical knowledge and understanding

Not all of the following need to be understood for any single device but all are relevant to the task:
- understanding of different types of spring systems (spiral tension or compression, torsion, bending-beam)
- understanding of centre of gravity, moments, pivots and friction (and possibly Istiction'), lever systems, parallel motion mechanisms
- knowledge and understanding of electronic sensors, including opto-devices, strain gauges, Hall effect devices, capacitive devices (in this case used with RF oscillators perhaps), LVDTS, potentiometers
- knowledge and understanding of transistors and operational amplifiers
- knowledge and understanding of electronic display devices, including analogue meters, 7-segment displays, LEDs and filament lamps
- knowledge of construction of simple spring systems or balancing beam sytems, manufacture of simple electronic circuits on PCBs or stripboard or matrix board.

© The Nuffield Foundation, 1997

Specialist tools, materials and equipment

- a range of elecronic components including transistors, op-amps, light sensors and small filament lamps
- PCB-making equipment or 'Veroboard' or similar to produce final circuit
- a selection of tension, compression and torsion springs
- piano wire of various gauges for making special springs
- spring steel strip or phosphor bronze strip for bending beams, or students could use acrylic or high impact polystyrene or similar provided deflection is kept small

- MDF, plastic, or aluminium sheet from which to make the mechanical parts of the device and equipment and tools for shaping these materials
- prototype boards, matrix board or systems kits for modelling, investigating and developing possible circuits are useful.

Cross-curricular links

maths

- calculations related to potential dividers, current gain, Ohm's law, centre-of-gravity, moments, Hook's Law.

science

- relevant concepts concerning Ohm's law, current, resistance potential difference, circuits, power sources, light, light sources, intensity, moments, balance, centre-of-gravity, springs, Hook's Law, magnetism, capacitance.

IT

- Crocodile Clips or similar software for developing circuits
- PCB designing software
- CAD for designing mechanical parts
- DTP and graphics for presentation of design work.

economic and industrial understanding

- economic and industrial understanding
- students can investigate the areas in school and in local shops, supermarkets, scrapyards and other places where weighing devices are used
- what principle of weighing is used?
- what user interfaces are involved and why and how they are used, and by how many people?

Useful Resource Tasks

To enable students to identify a situation where measuring weight is important:
- SRT 1 *Identifying needs and likes.*

To enable students to understand how a signal from a sensing device can be amplified and operate an output device which can be calibrated:
- SBRT 1 *Sensing an processing with transistors*
- SBRT 2 *Using a comparator*

- SBRT 5 *Circuits that count*
- IBRT 1 *Investigating transistor circuits*
- IBRT 2 *Investigating a comparator*
- IBRT 4 *Investigating counting.*

To appreciate factors involved in interfacing electronics to mechanical devices:
- MfRT 3 *Assembling an electromechanical system*
- ECRT 1 *Controlling a simple buggy*
- ECRT 2 *Choosing batteries.*

Useful Case Studies

- Measuring devices – exercise cycle
- Helping to keep air breathable.

Design brief

To design and make an electronic weighing machine to weigh small objects up to a mass of 250 g. The device should display the weight by either analogue or digital means and should have a means of 'zeroing, the display.

Preliminary specification

What the product should do:
- be able to weigh up to 250 g
- be able to weigh to an accuracy of at least +/–10 g
- have a means of adjusting output to zero when no weight is on the device
- have a means of calibrating the display.

Other features:
- it must run off batteries
- have facilities to replace the batteries

- no part of the device must over-heat
- the display may be either 'built-in' or remote
- it must not be damaged by 100% overload
- it must be simple for anyone to operate.

Possible optional features:
- it might sound a warning if the load is too great
- if designed for powders or liquids, it could incorporate an automatic loading and un-loading arrangement.

Design sketches

Principles of operation

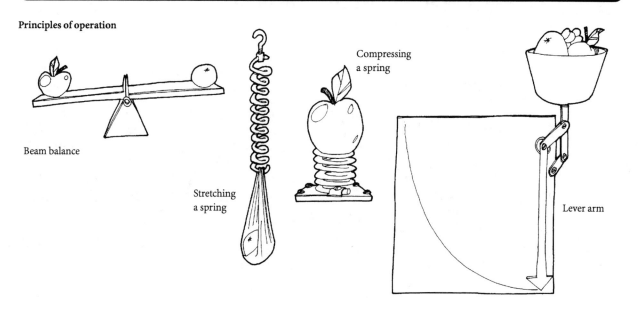

Beam balance

Stretching a spring

Compressing a spring

Lever arm

simple

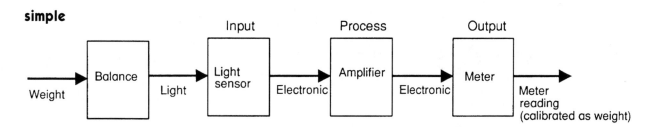

self-balancing

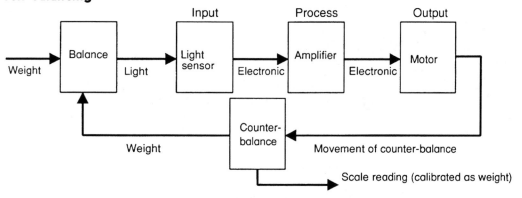

Information for making

simple

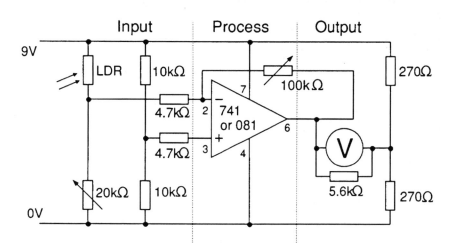

© The Nuffield Foundation, 1997

Information for making

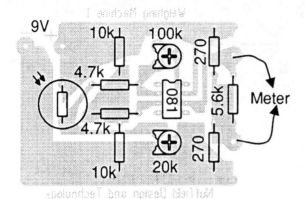

Weighing Machine 1

Nuffield Design and Technology

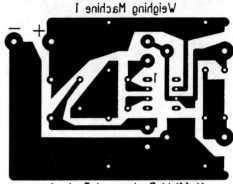

Weighing Machine 1

Nuffield Design and Technology

self-balancing

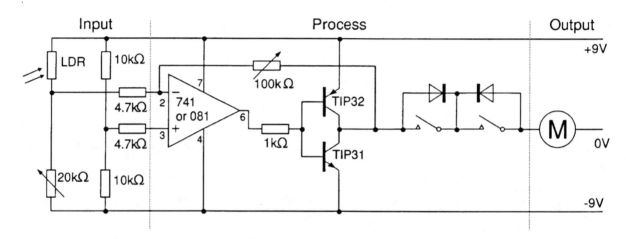

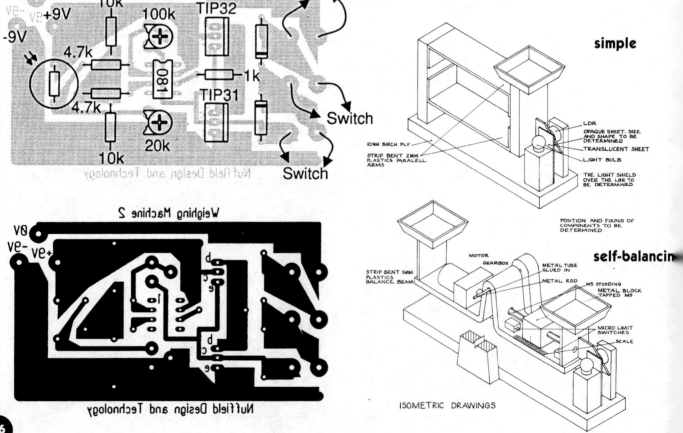

Weighing Machine 2

Nuffield Design and Technology

Weighing Machine 2

Nuffield Design and Technology

simple

self-balancing

ISOMETRIC DRAWINGS

Environment monitoring 4

A Capability Task for electronics
Line of interest – measuring devices

The task

To design and make a device that can measure environmental conditions such as light level, sound level or temperature.

Task setting

There are many occasions when it is useful to measure environmental conditions. Sound levels can rise dangerously high near heavy machinery and at pop concerts. Environmental health officers are concerned to limit noise pollution. Light levels are important for the growth of plants and when taking photographs. A potter needs to know the temperature in his or her kiln and a medical officer needs to know that the temperature in an old peoples' home is high enough to ward off hypothermia. In all these situations measuring environmental conditions is important. The students' task is to take a situation of their own choosing where such measuring would be useful and to design and make a device that can be used to take the measurements. Possibilties include a sound meter, a light meter and an electronic thermometer. The device will be used by a professional concerned with a particular environmental feature. It will be mass produced for sale through specialist professional equipment journals.

The aims of the task

- to enable students to identify a situation where measuring an environmental condition is important
- to enable students to identify which type of sensing device and output device would be most appropriate for the task
- to enable students to understand how a signal from a sensing device can be amplified and can operate an output device which can be calibrated
- to enable students to develop skills in designing and making a PCB and shell for the circuit and also a user guide.

Values

technical
Students should understand the environmental factors involved and the most appropriate way in which changes can be sensed.

economic
Students should appreciate the production methods which are appropriate for small-batch production.

aesthetic
Students should design a case for the product which is appropriate to the purpose of the device and the place where it will be used.

moral
Students should consider the issues involved in taking responsibility for the environment.

social
Students should consider issues related to keeping animals to provide company for those who live alone.

environmental
Students should consider the effects of a wide range of phenomena on the environment.

Nature of the product

This is a measuring device which will provide information about an environmental condition. The output signal may be read from a ready-made meter or on a purpose-built display. A more able student will calibrate the read out.

Technical knowledge and understanding

- knowledge of suitable sensors
- knowledge of suitable processing circuits
- knowledge of suitable output devices
- knowledge of PCB production
- knowledge of enclosure production techniques.

Specialist tools, materials and equipment

- a range of suitable sensors – thermistors, light-dependent resistors, microphones
- a range of suitable processors – op-amp ICs 741 or 3140 and, in the case of sound rectifying diodes, 1N4001
- a range of suitable output devices – simple DC meters, LED bar arrays.
- access to prototype boards or systems kits for modelling, investigating and developing possible circuits is useful

- PCB production facilities
  Possible suppliers:
  Maplin MPS on 01702 554000
  Rapid Electronics on 01206 751166
- vacuum forming facilities.

Cross-curricular links

maths
- calibration will involve use of scale and division.

science
- relevant concepts concerning the environmental factors which affect health and safety.

art
- using a scrap book for collecting images of the environment and situations in which the product could be used to inform the overall aesthetic of the device.

IT
- CAD software can be used to design the case and to produce the PCB layout.

geography
- the effect of human activity on the environment at local, regional and global levels.

economic and industrial understanding
- looking at the cost of environmental policies of a large company such as BT.

Useful Resource Tasks

To enable students to identify a situation where measuring an environmental condition is important:
- SRT 1 *Identifying needs and likes*
- SRT 2 *Questionnaires.*

To enable students to understand how a signal from a sensing device can be amplified and operate an output device which can be calibrated:
- SBRT 1 *Sensing and processing with transistors*
- SBRT 2 *Using a comparator*
- IBRT 1 *Investigating transistor circuits*
- IBRT 2 *Investigating a comparator.*

To enable students to develop skills in designing and making a PCB and shell for the circuit, and a user guide:
- CRT 4 *Communicating to the user*
- MfRT 2 *Making printed circuit boards*
- MfRT 4 *Producing enclosures.*

Useful Case Studies

To enable students to identify a situation where measuring an environmental condition is important:
- Helping to keep air breathable.

Design brief

To design and make a device that can measure environmental conditions, such as light level, sound level or temperature. It may be used by someone with a need to monitor the environment as part of their professional duties or by someone who has an interest in environmental affairs. It will be sold by a supplier specializing in environmental monitoring equipment and advertised in both trade journals and environmental-interest magazines.

Preliminary specification

What the product should do:
- measure an environmental condition, such as light level, sound level or temperature
- display the measurement in an easy-to-read form.

What the product should look like:
- suit the purpose of the device
- suit the location in which the product will be used.

Other features:
- simple to operate
- powered by a battery
- have an ON/OFF switch
- have facilities to replace the battery
- be suitable for small-batch production.

Design sketches

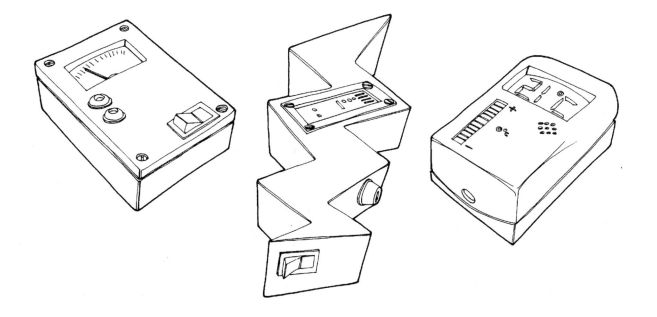

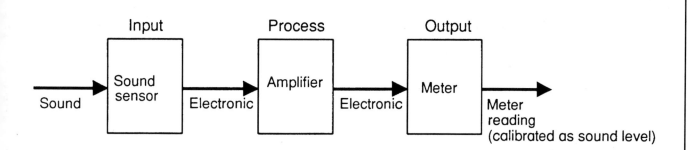

Input	Process	Output
Sound sensor	Amplifier	Meter

Sound → Sound sensor → Electronic → Amplifier → Electronic → Meter → Meter reading (calibrated as sound level)

Information for making

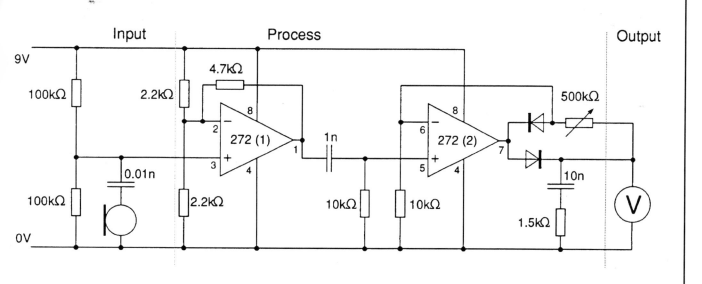

© The Nuffield Foundation, 1997

Information for making

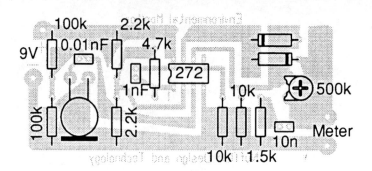

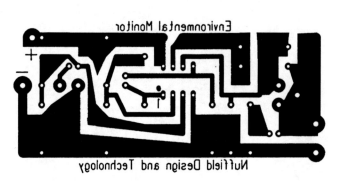

FIRST ANGLE ORTHOGRAPHIC PROJECTION

EXPLODED ISOMETRIC DRAWING

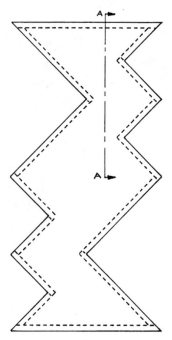

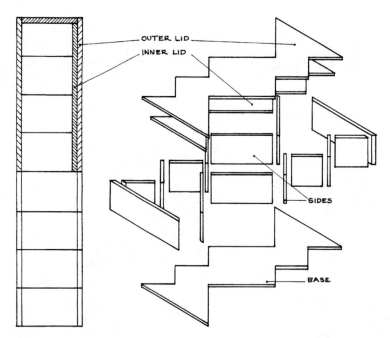

FRONT ELEVATION

PART SECTIONAL END
ELEVATION ON A A

CONSTRUCTED FROM SHEET MATERIAL
BUTT JOINTED AND GLUED
PAINTED FINISH
SIZES AND POSITION OF COMPONENTS
TO BE DECIDED

Light and sound 5

A Capability Task for electronics
Line of interest – electronic novelties

The task

To design and make a quality prototype version of an electronic novelty, utilizing either light or sound effects, which is suitable for batch production.

Task setting

The production of sound and light effects is easily achieved with simple electronic systems. The student's task here is to utilize this technical capability to develop an electronic novelty that will appeal to a particular user group.

The aims of the task

- to enable students to analyse a potential commercial design opportunity and evaluate existing products to inform their designing and making
- to develop an understanding of timer and counter circuits and their opportunities

- to teach the communication techniques needed to describe the product and how to use it to potential customers
- to enable students to develop high quality making skills and to consider manufacturing issues in their designing, particularly in relation to batch-production techniques using thermoplastic.

Values

technical
Students should consider the need for accuracy, precision and finish in the design and construction of the novelty.

economic
Students should consider the risks involved in tooling up for the mass production of a product which may rapidly lose appeal.

aesthetic
Students should consider the overall style of the product in terms of its appeal to potential customers.

moral
Students should attempt to reconcile the application of valuable resources for desirable, yet essentially frivolous, uses.

social
Students should consider the influence of peer group pressure on the acceptability and status of novelty items.

environmental
At the design stage students should consider the potential for recycling the materials to be used.

Nature of the product

There is a wide variety of possible products, for example:
- special effects sound makers
- door chimes
- simple musical instrument
- seasonal light up displays
- light-up jewellery.

For some of these dedicated ICs are available; others can be developed from standard components. Whatever product is developed, it is important that the item produced is considered from both aesthetic and technical viewpoints.

Technical knowledge and understanding

- knowledge of standard timer and counter ICs to create sound and light effects
- knowledge of specialist ICs for sound and light effects
- knowledge of suitable amplification circuits and output devices
- knowledge of enclosure production techniques suitable for batch production
- understanding of ergonomic considerations in respect of design for worn or hand-held objects.

Specialist tools, materials and equipment

- access to a range of electronic components, including timer and counter ICs, resistors, capacitors, transistors, buzzers, speakers and LEDs
- access to prototype boards or systems kits for modelling, investigating and developing possible circuits is useful

- PCB production facilities
  Possible suppliers:
  Maplin MPS on 01702 554000
  Rapid Electronics on 01206 751166
- vacuum forming facilities.

© The Nuffield Foundation, 1997

Cross-curricular links

maths
- using formulae to calculate time constants and frequencies.

science
- relevant concepts concerning choice of material for novelty items – colour, durability, ease of cleaning, ease of gripping.

art
- observational drawings of contemporary graphic art themes related to current fashions and trends.

IT
- CAD software can be used to design enclosures and to produce the PCB layout
- simulation software, such as Crocodile Clips , can be used to develop the electronics by adding further building blocks, such as an astable for output.

economic and industrial understanding
- design consideration related to batch production techniques.

Useful Resource Tasks

To enable students to analyse a potential commercial design opportunity and evaluate existing products to inform their designing and making:
- SRT 1 *Identifying needs and wants*
- SRT 4 *Brainstorming*.

To develop an understanding of timer and counter circuits and their opportunities:
- SBRT 3 *Introducing timing into circuits*
- SBRT 5 *Circuits that count*
- IBRT 3 *Designing timing circuits*
- IBRT 5 *Investigating counting*.

To teach the communication techniques needed to describe the product and how to use it to potential customers:
- CRT 1 *Communicating ideas to the client*
- CRT 4 *Communicating to the user*.

To enable students to develop high quality making skills and to consider manufacturing issues in their designing, particularly related to batch-production techniques using thermoplastic:
- MfRT 4 *Producing enclosures*.

Useful Case Studies

To enable students to analyse a potential commercial design opportunity and evaluate existing products to inform their designing and making:

- Electronic novelties – 'soft' noise making toys.

Design brief

To design and make a quality prototype version of an electronic novelty utilizing either light or sound effects. It is envisaged that the item will be available from a range of retail and mail order outlets, depending on the nature of the novelty The product should be suitable for batch production.

Preliminary specification

Electronic organ

What the product should do:
- produce a range of musical notes in a scale
- allow the playing of simple melodies through a keyboard.

What it should look like:
- be attractive and appealing to the target group.

Other features:
- powered from a battery
- have an ON/OFF switch
- have facilities to replace the battery
- suitable for small-batch production from thermoplastic
- meet all relevant EU safety standards.

Electronic jewellery

What the product should do:
- produce a changing light visual display within a piece of jewellery or body adornment
- have an ergonomically comfortable design

What it should look like:
- be attractive and appealing to the target group.

Other features:
- powered from a battery
- have an ON/OFF switch
- have facilities to replace the battery
- suitable for small-batch production from thermoplastic
- meet all relevant EU safety standards.

Design sketches

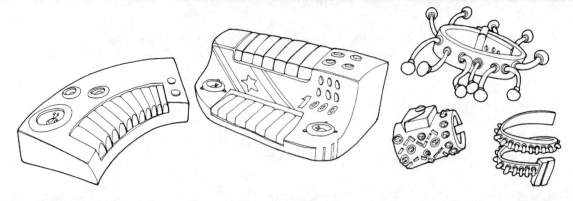

Electronic organ

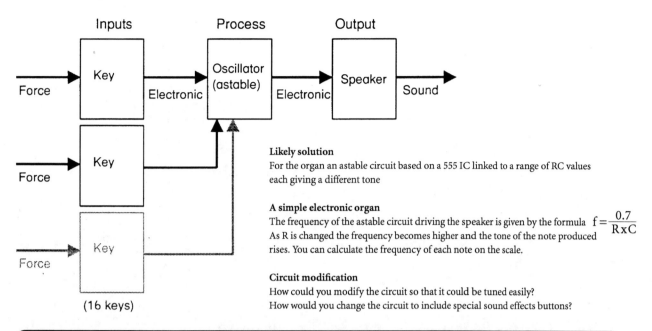

Inputs

Key — Force

Key — Force

Key — Force

(16 keys)

Electronic

Process

Oscillator (astable)

Electronic

Output

Speaker — Sound

Likely solution
For the organ an astable circuit based on a 555 IC linked to a range of RC values each giving a different tone

A simple electronic organ
The frequency of the astable circuit driving the speaker is given by the formula $f = \dfrac{0.7}{R \, x \, C}$
As R is changed the frequency becomes higher and the tone of the note produced rises. You can calculate the frequency of each note on the scale.

Circuit modification
How could you modify the circuit so that it could be tuned easily?
How would you change the circuit to include special sound effects buttons?

Information for making
Electronic organ

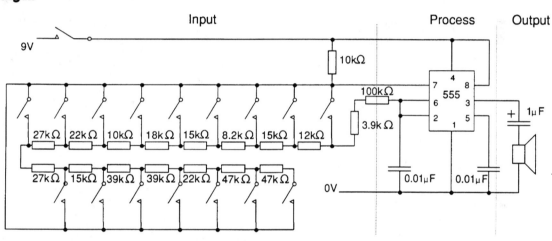

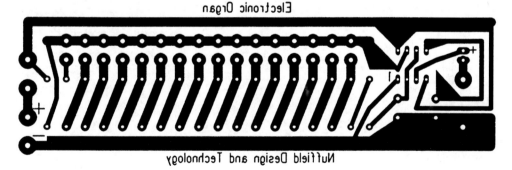

Electronic Organ

Nuffield Design and Technology

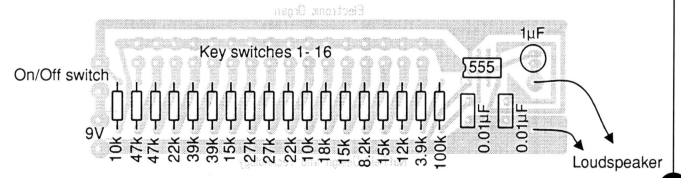

On/Off switch

Key switches 1- 16

9V

10k 47k 47k 22k 39k 39k 15k 27k 27k 22k 10k 18k 15k 8.2k 15k 12k 3.9k 100k

0.01µF 0.01µF

1µF

555

Loudspeaker

Design sketches

Electronic jewellery

Simple chaser jewellery
The LEDs light up in a rapid sequence as the astable pulses the counter and it counts up and then down.

Outputs
(multiple LEDs)

Force → [Input — Switch] —Electronic→ [Process — Oscillator (astable)] —Electronic→ [Process — Counter] —Electronic→ [LED] → Light

[LED] → Light

Information for making

Electronic jewellery

For up to five LEDs an ic (2050) that combines the oscillator and counter can be used

R1: 150kΩ to 300kΩ. This determines the flash rate
mode: select sequence or random flashing

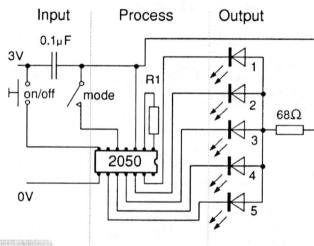

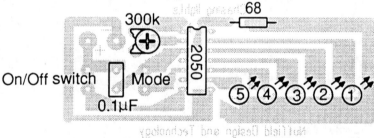

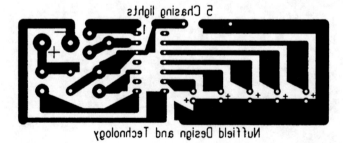

Circuit modification
How would you change the circuit so that it included sound as well as light?

Product modification
How would you change the overall form of the product so that it was more dramatic?

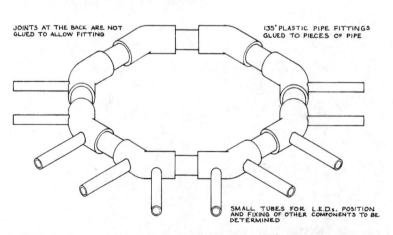

The task

To design and make a quality prototype version of a hand-held travel game suitable for batch production.

Task setting

Travelling to holiday destinations in far-off places offers excitement and reward at the journey's end. However, hours spent waiting for delayed flights or in endless summer traffic jams can be a misery. This is particularly true when travelling with young children. Travel games and puzzles offer parents respite from fractious children. Traditional forms of these skill challenge games, such as a marble maze. have been replaced by electronic game boxes.

Electronic Novelties Incorporated has identified the opportunity to produce a new range of travel games. These will combine the fun of traditional skill challenge with the flashy reward of sound and light associated with contemporary electronic game boxes.

The aims of the task

- to enable students to analyse a potential commercial design opportunity and evaluate existing products to inform their designing and making
- to develop an understanding of monostable timer circuits and their opportunities

- to teach the communication techniques needed to describe the parts and assembly of an electronic product
- to enable students to develop high quality making skills and to consider manufacturing issues in their designing, particularly related to batch-production techniques using thermoplastic.

Values

technical
Students should consider the need for accuracy and precision in the design and construction of a small hand-held travel game.

economic
Students should consider the risks involved in tooling up for the mass production of a product which may rapidly lose appeal.

aesthetic
Students should consider the overall style of the product in terms of its appeal to potential customers.

moral
Students should attempt to reconcile the application of valuable resources for desirable, yet essentially frivolous, uses.

social
Students should consider the merits of manufacturing products which promote solitary and potentially anti-social leisure activity; for example, computer games.

environmental
At the design stage, students should consider the potential for recycling the materials to be used.

Nature of the product

In its simplest form, the product will consist of a maze-type challenge to be completed against the monostable time delay. This offers a variety of thermoplastic case design opportunities allied to developing an understanding of the timer circuit.

Scope for electronic development exists through research into, and incorporation of, additional building block circuits:

- an astable circuit for flashing lights or imaginative sounds
- a variety of clock and counter opportunities for digital time delay
- logic opportunities, such as five balls in their sequentially correct maze positions sets output.

Technical knowledge and understanding

- knowledge of transistor and timer ICs to create monostable timer circuits capable of giving time on and time off delays
- knowledge of timing ICs and associated circuits
- knowledge of suitable processing circuits
- knowledge of suitable output devices

- knowledge of enclosure production techniques suitable for batch production
- understanding of ergonomic considerations in respect of design for hand-held objects.

© The Nuffield Foundation, 1997

Specialist tools, materials and equipment

- access to a range of electronic components, including timer ICs, resistors, capacitors, transistors, buzzers, speakers and LEDs
- access to prototype boards or systems kits for modelling, investigating and developing possible circuits is useful

- PCB production facilities
  Possible suppliers:
  Maplin MPS on 01702 554000
  Rapid Electronics on 01206 751166
- vacuum forming facilities.

Cross-curricular links

maths

- using RC formula to calculate the monostable time constant.

science

- relevant concepts concerning choice of material for hand-held game – colour, durability, ease of cleaning, ease of gripping.

art

- observational drawings of contemporary graphic art themes related to current fashions and trends.

IT

- CAD software can be used to design the case and to produce the PCB layout
- simulation software, such as Crocodile Clips , can be used to develop the electronics by adding further building blocks, such as an astable for output
- CAD software can be used to design the case and produce the PCB.

economic and industrial understanding

- design consideration related to batch-production techniques.

Useful Resource Tasks

To enable students to analyse a potential commercial design opportunity and evaluate existing products to inform their designing and making:
- SRT 2 *Questionnaires*
- SRT 5 *Attribute analysis.*

To develop an understanding of monostable timer circuits and their opportunities:
- SBRT 3 *Introducing timing into circuits*
- IBRT 3 *Designing timing circuits*

To teach the communication techniques needed to describe the parts and assembly of an electronic product:
- CRT 2 *Communiating ideas to the maker 1*
- CRT 3 *Communiating ideas to the maker 2.*

To enable students to develop high quality making skills and to consider manufacturing issues in their designing, particularly related to batch-production techniques using thermoplastic:
- MfRT4 *Producing enclosures.*

Useful Case Studies

To enable students to analyse a potential commercial design opportunity and evaluate existing products to inform their designing and making:
- Electronic novelties – 'soft' noise making toys.

Design brief

To design and prototype an electronic hand-held travel game suitable for eight to twelve year-olds. It is envisaged that the item will be available from motorway service stations and airport shops. The product should be suitable for batch production.

Preliminary specification

What the product should do:
- provide challenging amusement for children in the age range of eight to twelve, while travelling
- offer a manipulative skill challenge with an electronic visual or audible reward output.

What the product should look like:
- a compact and self-contained robust, travel-sized product
- be attractive and appealing to the target group
- be an ergonomically comfortable design for the specified age range.

Other features:
- powered from a battery
- have an ON/OFF switch
- have facilities to replace the battery
- be suitable for small batch production from thermoplastic
- cost no more than £7.99, including the cost of the case
- meet all relevant EU safety standards.

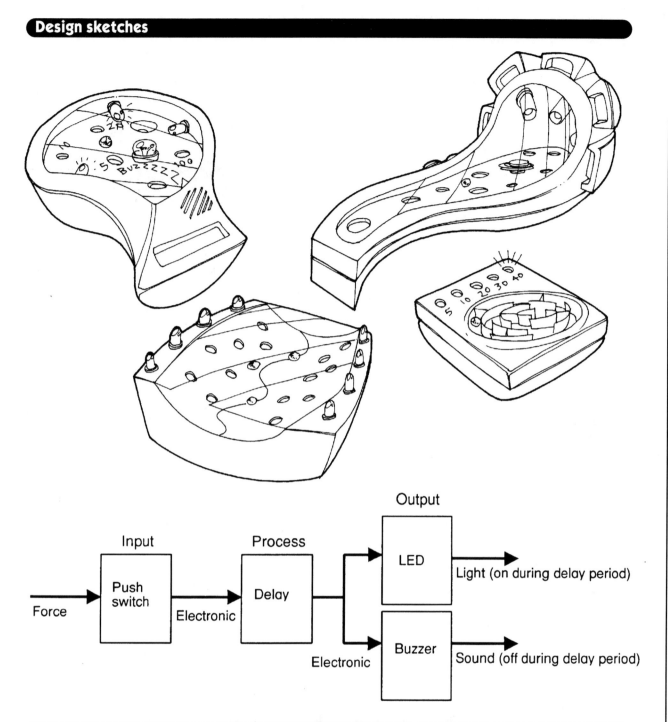

Information for making

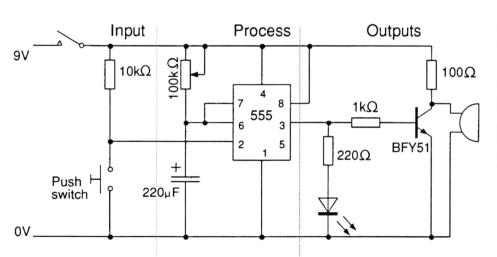

Likely solution
A monostable circuit based on a 555 IC

A basic limited time to play circuit

Circuit modification
How would you change the circuit to provide a reward when the player 'beats the clock'?

Information for making

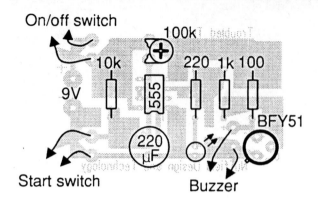

On/off switch

10k

9V

100k

220 1k 100

555

220 μF

BFY51

Start switch

Buzzer

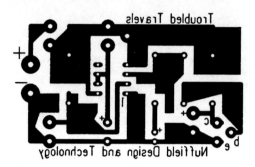

A basic enclosure

This is made from a shell of polystyrene, produced by vacuum forming, fitting over a simple base, inside which fit the battery and circuit. Level of difficulty dial is simply the shaft of a variable resistor coming through the side of the base.

Enclosure modification

How would you change the shape of the base so that it is more comfortable to hold and make the level of difficulty dial more interesting and accessible?

PLAN

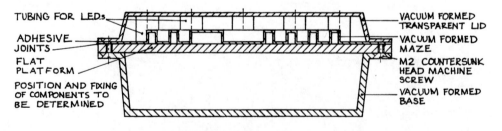

TUBING FOR LEDs

ADHESIVE JOINTS

FLAT PLATFORM

POSITION AND FIXING OF COMPONENTS TO BE DETERMINED

VACUUM FORMED TRANSPARENT LID

VACUUM FORMED MAZE

M2 COUNTERSUNK HEAD MACHINE SCREW

VACUUM FORMED BASE

SECTION ON AA

THIRD ANGLE ORTHOGRAPHIC PROJECTION

Lock it up

A Capability Task for electronics
Line of interest – security systems

The task

To design and construct an electronic lock.

Task setting

Normal locks which have keys are useful, but there is still the problem of keeping the key safe and the risk of losing it. The task for the student is to design and construct an electronic lock which uses logic gates to operate a suitable output in the form of a solenoid (or relay plus solenoid) operating as a locking bar. The device could be fitted to a box or cupboard where this level of security is required.

The aims of the task

- to enable students to identify situations where an electronic lock might be used
- to enable students to understand and use logic gates for decision making
- to enable students to understand and use a solenoid for mechanical purposes
- to enable students to develop skills in designing and making a PCB for the circuit and also a production guide.

Values

technical
Students should consider the working conditions for the device, the need for compactness, tamper proofing and the possibility of remote operation.

economic
Students should consider the relationship between production methods and the scale of production and how this might influence appearance.

aesthetic
Students should consider how the appearance of the case might be appropriate to the purpose of the device and to the place where it will be used.

moral
Students should consider whether stealing can ever be justified and the lengths to which people are entitled to go in order to protect property.

social
Students should consider alternative methods of preventing theft – the notion of 'designing out crime'.

environmental
High security environments are often intimidating and anonymous; students should consider the sort of environment that protects valuables without alienating.

Nature of the product

This is an electronic lock which is operated by the output of a set of logic gates. Input to the gates is by the use of push switches. When the final output is high, a solenoid will operate, causing the lock to open. Options include:

- correct switches in any sequence to operate the lock
- including dummy switches which, if pressed, prevent unlocking
- switches must be pushed in a particular sequence
- dummy switches that are not connected, to make the sequence harder to guess
- mounting the switches in the form of a key-pad
- a lock out facility to prevent the door from opening if any of the dummy switches are pressed
- if any incorrect switches are pressed, an alarm to warn that an unauthorised person is using the lock
- an automatic reset which operates when the door is opened and closed.

Technical knowledge and understanding

- knowledge of suitable input devices, such as simple-to-make key-pad and latching push switches
- knowledge of processing devices, such as logic gates and the way in which they can be connected
- knowledge of suitable output devices, such as solenoids and relays
- knowledge of current drain and battery capacity.

© The Nuffield Foundation, 1997

Specialist tools, materials and equipment

- a range of logic gate ICs, such as Quad AND gate IC 4018B, quad NOR gate IC 4001
- a range of DIL IC holders
- suitable solenoids
- a range of relays with sufficient contacts to allow the relay to be latched
- latching push switches
- springs and small sections of mild steel or aluminium to allow a return device to be constructed

- facilities for working metal
- access to prototype boards or systems kits for modelling, investigating and developing possible circuits is useful
- PCB production facilities
  Possible suppliers:
  Maplin MPS on 01702 554000
  Rapid Electronics on 01206 751166.

Cross-curricular links

maths
- truth tables
- measurements of operating and quiescent current drain can be used to calulate likely battery life.

science
- relevant concepts concerning the properties of materials which make them suitable for security devices – strength, stiffness, resistance to abrasion and corrosion.

art
- sketch books exploring images related to protection, denying access and prevention could be used to inform the overall aesthetic of the device.

IT
- CAD software can be used to design the case and to produce the PCB layout.

economic and industrial understanding
- looking at the cost of small thefts, such as shoplifting and petty pilfering, from a variety of standpoints.

Useful Resource Tasks

To enable students to identify situations where an electronic lock might be used:
- SRT 2 *Questionnaires.*

To enable students to develop skills in producing a production guide:
- CRT 2 *Communicating ideas to the maker 1*
- CRT 3 *Communicating ideas to the maker 2.*

To enable students to understand and use logic gates for decision making:
- CCRT 1 *Component sorting*
- SBRT 4 *Combining signals*
- IBRT 4 *Designing logic circuits.*

To enable students to develop skills in designing and making a PCB:
- MfRT 2 *Making printed circuit boards.*

Useful Case Studies

To enable students to identify situations where an electronic lock might be used:
- Security devices – intruder alarm for cars.

Design brief

To design and make an electronic lock which can be used for a box or cupboard or for a room door. It will be bought by anyone who wishes to keep something safe and who does not want to run the risk of losing a key. It would be on sale in a shop which sells locks and security devices.

Preliminary specification

What the product should do:
- provide an effective lock for a box, cupboard or room.

What the product should look like:
- be concealed from view inside the box, cupboard or room it is protecting
- be enclosed in a case
- suit the purpose of the device
- suit the location in which the product will be used.

Other features:
- utilize a solenoid
- be powered from a battery
- have facilities to replace the battery
- be suitable for small-batch production
- cost no more than £15.50, including the cost of the case.

Design sketches

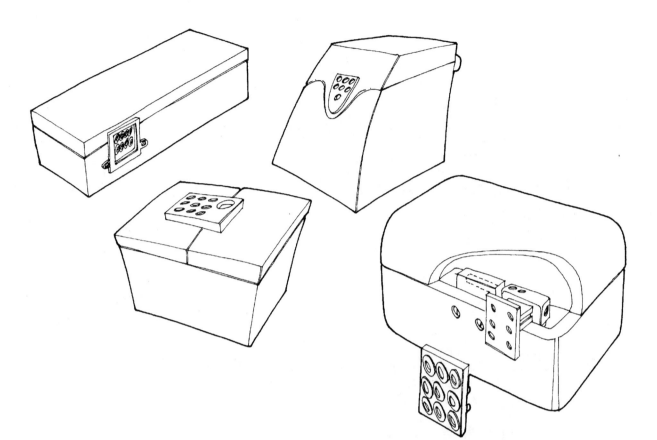

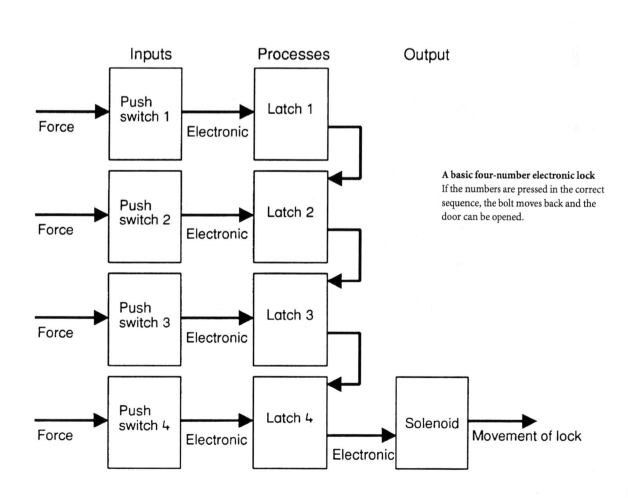

A basic four-number electronic lock
If the numbers are pressed in the correct
sequence, the bolt moves back and the
door can be opened.

Information for making

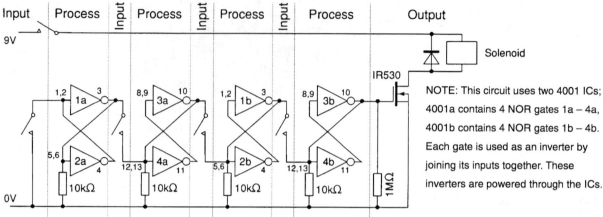

NOTE: This circuit uses two 4001 ICs; 4001a contains 4 NOR gates 1a – 4a, 4001b contains 4 NOR gates 1b – 4b. Each gate is used as an inverter by joining its inputs together. These inverters are powered through the ICs.

Likely solution

This solution is based on the electronic lock found in TEP Control pages 29–40. It uses an FET transistor to drive the solenoid, a diode to protect this transistor for back EMF, and a minimum of external components with two 4001 quad NOR gate ICs to provide a lock that requires sequential input to release the solenoid. A key switch is used to engage the lock and a key-pad is used to open it.

Circuit modification

If any incorrect switches are pressed, how would you incorporate an alarm to warn that an unauthorized person is using the lock?

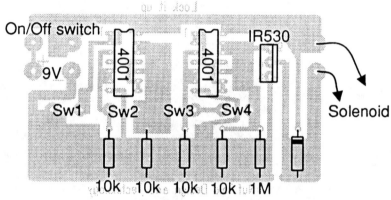

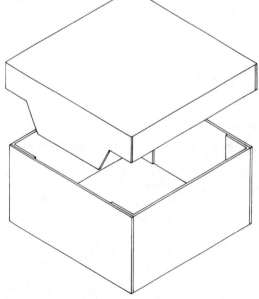

EXPLODED ISOMETRIC DRAWING OF THE BOX AND LID

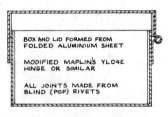

BOX AND LID FORMED FROM FOLDED ALUMINIUM SHEET

MODIFIED MAPLIN'S YL04E HINGE OR SIMILAR

ALL JOINTS MADE FROM BLIND (POP) RIVETS

CROSS SECTION THROUGH THE HINGED BOX AND LID

A basic enclosure

The case is made from 0.8-mm aluminium sheet, with the corners joined by pop rivets.

© The Nuffield Foundation, 1997

Safe and sound (8)

The task

To design and construct a tamper alarm for a sports back or school bag.

Task setting

It is often important to know if someone else is interfering with your personal possessions. The task for the student is to design and construct a tamper alarm for a bag, which makes use of a silicon controlled rectifier and a suitable audible output operated by a tilt switch. The device will be used by students who wished to have a tamper alarm fitted to their bag and is designed as a one-off product.

The aims of the task

- to enable students to identify situations where an alarm system might be used
- to enable students to identify which type of sensing device and output device would be most appropriate for the task
- to enable students to understand how a signal from a sensing device can be amplified and can operate an output device
- to enable students to develop skills in designing and making a PCB for the circuit and also a shell and a user guide.

Values

technical

Students should consider the working conditions for the device, particularly the need to withstand rough handling.

economic

Students should consider the relationship between production methods and the scale of production and how this might influence appearance.

aesthetic

Students should consider how the appearance of the case might be appropriate to the purpose of the device and to the place where it will be used.

moral

Students should consider whether stealing can ever be justified and the lengths to which people are entitled to go in order to protect property.

social

Students should consider alternative methods of preventing theft – the notion of 'designing out crime'.

environmental

Students should consider a time limit on the length of time for which the alarm sounds.

Nature of the product

This is a sensing device for a school or sports bag which will operate an alarm signal if the bag is tampered with. The output signal should stay on once operated. A more able student might develop a range of possible output signals.

Technical knowledge and understanding

- knowledge of suitable sensors
- knowledge of suitable processing circuits
- knowledge of suitable output devices
- knowledge of production techniques
- knowledge of enclosure production techniques.

Specialist tools, materials and equipment

- a range of suitable sensors – tilt switch, trembler switch, light-dependent resistors
- a range of suitable output devices – buzzers, bells, siren circuits plus loudspeakers
- latching processors – BFY51 and BC108 transistors plus relays, silicon controlled rectifier
- access to prototype boards or systems kits for modelling, investigating and developing possible circuits is useful

- PCB production facilities
  Possible suppliers:
  Maplin MPS on 01702 554000
  Rapid Electronics on 01206 751166
- vacuum forming facilities.

Cross-curricular links

maths
- calculating the cost of different alternative circuits.

science
- relevant concepts concerning the properties of materials which make them suitable for security devices – strength, stiffness, resistance to abrasion and corrosion.

art
- sketch books exploring the appearance of everyday objects which could be used to disguise or contain a tamper alarm.

IT
- CAD software can be used to design the case and to produce the PCB layout.

economic and industrial understanding
- looking at the cost of small thefts, such as shoplifting and petty pilfering, from a variety of standpoints.

Useful Resource Tasks

To enable students to identify situations where an alarm system might be used:
- SRT 2 *Questionnaires*.

To enable students to develop skills in designing and producing a user guide:
- CRT 4 *Communicating to the user*.

To enable students to understand how a signal from a sensing device can be amplified and can operate an output device:
- CCRT 1 *Component sorting*
- SBRT 1 *Sensing and processing with transistors*
- IBRT 1 *Investigating transistor circuits*.

To enable students to develop skills in designing and making a PCB for the circuit:
- MfRT 1 *Making circuit layouts using copper tape (suitable for less able students)*
- MfRT 2 *Making printed circuit boards*.

Useful Case Studies

To enable students to identify situations where an alarm system might be used:
- Security devices – intruder alarm for cars.

Design brief

To design and make an alarm system for a sports or school bag which will sound if the bag is tampered with. This could be connected to the zip fastening, or operated by a tilt switch. It will be bought by the owner of the bag or, perhaps in the case of a younger child, by a parent. It would be on sale in a shop which sells bags and suitcases.

Preliminary specification

What the product should do:
- sound an audible alarm when the bag is tampered with
- continue to sound until reset, or for a defined time period.

What the product should look like:
- suit the purpose of the device
- suit the location in which the product will be used (it may be disguised).

Other features:
- easily armed and disarmed by the owner
- not easily disarmed by others
- powered from a battery
- have facilities to replace the battery
- cost no more than £9.50, including the cost of the case.

Design sketches

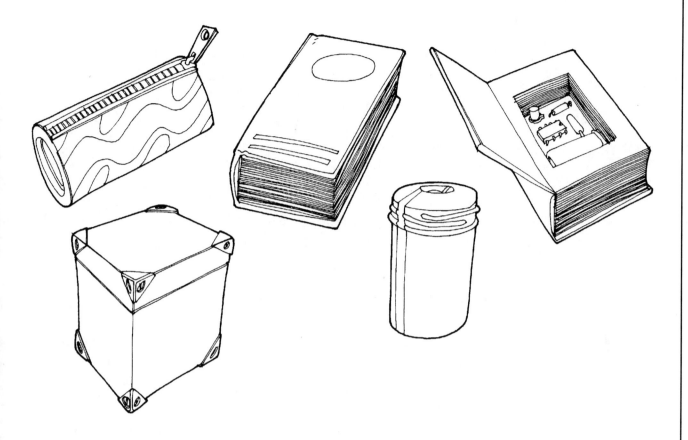

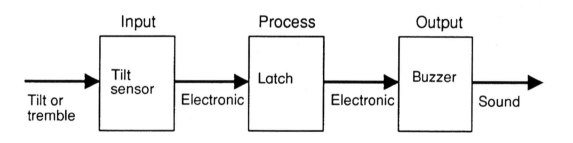

Information for making

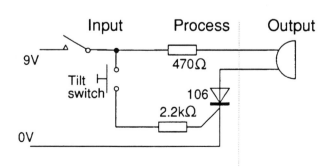

Likely solution
An SCR based circuit operated by a suitable switch, and operating a suitable buzzer or other audible alarm.

Basic tamper alarm system
The buzzer will sound when the operating switch is ON.

Circuit modification
How would you modify the output device so that a wailing siren sound is produced ?

© The Nuffield Foundation, 1997

Information for making

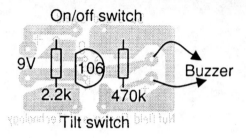

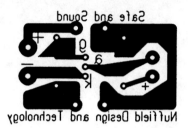

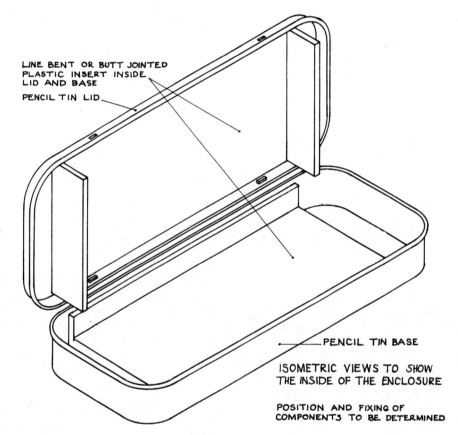

LINE BENT OR BUTT JOINTED
PLASTIC INSERT INSIDE
LID AND BASE

PENCIL TIN LID

PENCIL TIN BASE

ISOMETRIC VIEWS TO SHOW
THE INSIDE OF THE ENCLOSURE

POSITION AND FIXING OF
COMPONENTS TO BE DETERMINED

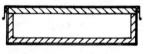

A CROSS SECTION
THROUGH THE ENCLOSURE

A basic enclosure

The case is made from an actual pencil tin with a lining constructed
from flat sheets of polystyrene glued together.

Enclosure modification

Consider how you might develop a kit which allows the purchaser to
integrate the tamper device into the fabric of a fabric pencil case.

Display system

9

A Capability Task for electronics
Line of interest – electronic control systems

The task

To design and make a moving display for a museum or exhibition, to explain how an industrial or commercial activity takes place.

Task setting

Moving displays are often used to explain complex processes in museums and exhibitions. Even with the advent of virtual reality displays, working models still have an attraction and appeal. There are many industrial/commercial activities which lend themselves to explanation by moving display, such as:

- coal mining
- steel making
- electricity generation in a nuclear power station
- the workings of a container port
- car manufacture
- textile production.

The student's task is to identify an area of industrial or commercial activity which lends itself to explanation by moving display and then to design and construct the display, complete with an electronic control system to keep it in motion.

The aims of the task

- to reinforce the technique of electronic design through a systems approach with an understanding of feedback
- to enable students to utilize programmable logic controller ICs
- to investigate various types of sensing devices and circuits
- to appreciate the factors involved in interfacing electronics to mechanical devices

- to develop communication skills
- to develop high quality electronic, mechanical and model making skills.

Values

technical
Students should consider the advantages and disadvantages of different control methods.

economic
Students should consider the sources of funding for exhibitions and museums.

aesthetic
Students should consider the importance of detail in the appearance of their display.

moral
Students should consider the possible effects of displays and exhibitions on public perception of industrial/commercial activity.

social
Students should consider the role that museums and exhibitions play in the way people use their leisure time.

environmental
Students should consider how they show environmental aspects of the industrial/commercial activity they are displaying.

Nature of the product

This is a completely automated display of an area of industrial or commercial activity as chosen by the student. This could be a large and complex task, in which case it is suitable for a team of students in which each student is responsible for a particular feature of the display and the team as a whole is responsible for integrating each feature into the overall display. There is the very real opportunity of working closely with a local industry and producing a display that is the centrepiece of their main reception area. The control functions within the display will lend themselves to the use of programmable logic controller ICs.

Technical knowledge and understanding

- use of programmable logic controller ICs, such as TEP PLC IC or Nottingham Trent University ICON PLC IC
- how to provide inputs into PLC ICs from a variety of sensors
- how to provide outputs from PLC ICs which will drive LEDs, lamps and motors
- use of simple electromechanical systems.

Specialist tools, materials and equipment

Each working display will require the following:
- a range of electronic components including transistors, op-amps, light sensors, reed switches, micro switches, LEDs, small filament lamps
- several small 6V DC motors (or, for more advanced variations, stepper motors) plus gears or pulleys
- PLC ICs plus programming software and computer
- access to prototype boards or systems kits for modelling, investigating and developing possible circuits is useful.

Possible suppliers:
Maplin MPS on 01702 554000
Rapid Electronics on 01206 751166
Teaching Resources, Middlesex University 0181 447 0342
ICON Project Nottingham Trent University 0115 941 8418.

Cross-curricular links

maths
- use of scale in developing the dimensions of the display
- calculations related to rotational speed and gear/pulley ratios.

science
- relevant concepts in electricity, magnetism and mechanics to produce simple working models.

art
- observational sketching of the industrial/commercial setting will be essential.

IT
- use of controller software for PLC.

economical and industrial understanding
- students can investigate the economic performance of the industrial/commercial activity.

Useful Resource Tasks

To reinforce the technique of electronic design through a systems approach with an understanding of feedback and to enable students to utilize programmable logic controller ICs:
- PICRT 1 *Using microcontrollers*
- PICRT 2 *Comparing simple programmable and hard-wired systems*
- PICRT 3 *Developing sophisticated systems.*

To investigate various types of sensing devices and circuits:
- SBRT 1 *Sensing and processing with transistors*
- IBRT 1 *Investigating transistor circuits.*

To develop communication skills:
- CRT 1 *Communicating ideas to the client*
- CRT 2 *Communicating ideas to the maker 1*
- CRT 3 *Communicating ideas to the maker 2.*

To develop high quality electronic, mechanical and model making skills; to appreciate factors involved in interfacing electronics to mechanical devices; to develop high quality electronic and mechanical making skills:
- MfRT 3 *Assembling an electromechanical system*
- CCRT 1 *Controlling a simple buggy.*

Useful Case Studies

To reinforce the technique of electronic design through a systems approach with an understanding of feedback:
- Communicating devices – bus arrival times system, the countdown service

- Helping to keep air breathable.

Design brief

To design and make a moving display for a museum or exhibition to explain how an industrial or commercial activity takes place. The display should be attractive, with the possibility of use as a centrepiece in a main reception area. It should operate automatically.

Preliminary specification

What the product should do:
- show clearly the key features of an industrial or commercial activity by means of a moving display
- operate automatically.

What the product should look like:
- provide a realistic, detailed and well-finished impression of the industrial/commercial activity.

Other possible features:
- operates only after someone pushes a start button
- stops after, say, 30 seconds and requires re-start
- includes taped commentary which plays while the display is operating.

Design sketches

Here we depart from the usual format and produce a list of control questions which teachers can use with students in looking at the containerization scene.

In your display ...

- How will the lorry know when to stop?
- How will the crane sense that the lorry has arrived?
- How the crane sense when it has gripped the container?
- How will the crane know how high to lift the container?
- How will the crane know where to place the container?
- How will the crane know when the container is in place?
- How will the crane know when to release the container?
- How will the crane know when to move off?
- How many lorries will you have in operation?
- How does each one know where to go?
- Could they be on a turntable?

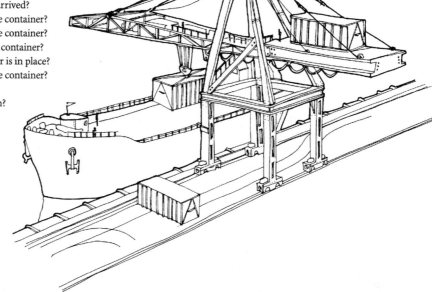

Information for making

Connections to the TEP PLC

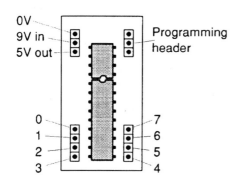

0 – 7 are the eight input/output connections. These are outputs until set as an input by a PLC program.

Typical use

Connecting a single input (push switch) to line 3 and a single output (LED) to line 5.

Connections to PIC ICs

There are many PIC chips; this shows the connections to two of them

12672

1 – 5V
2 – input or output
3 – input with analogue to digital convertor or output
4 – input
5 – input with analogue to digital convertor or output
6 – input with analogue to digital convertor or output
7 – input with analogue to digital convertor or output
8 – 0V

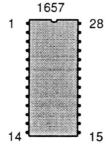

1657

Summary of connections:

2 – 5V
4 – 0V
6 to 25 – input or output (20 lines)

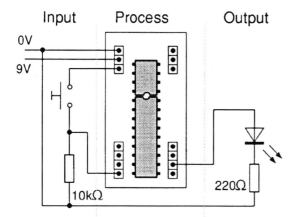

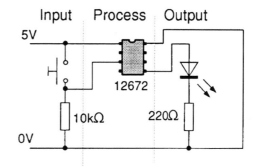

NOTES:

1. The way these circuits work is controlled by the program in the chip.
2. Make sure that the process chips are protected from high currents.

SIDE VIEW

PULLEY   DRIVE BELT

BOGIE

MOTOR AND GEARBOX TO MOVE THE DRIVE BELT

BOGIE WHICH CARRIES A MOTOR AND GEARBOX FOR THE LIFTING TACKLE

TWO OF EACH STRUCTURAL MEMBER ARE CUT FROM BIRCH PLYWOOD AND GLUED

MICRO SWITCH TO SENSE THE LIMIT OF TRAVEL OF MODEL AND OF BOGIE ON JIB

BASE OF LEG AND GEARBOX

PLAN VIEW

ISOMETRIC DRAWING

POSITION AND FIXING OF COMPONENTS TO BE DETERMINED

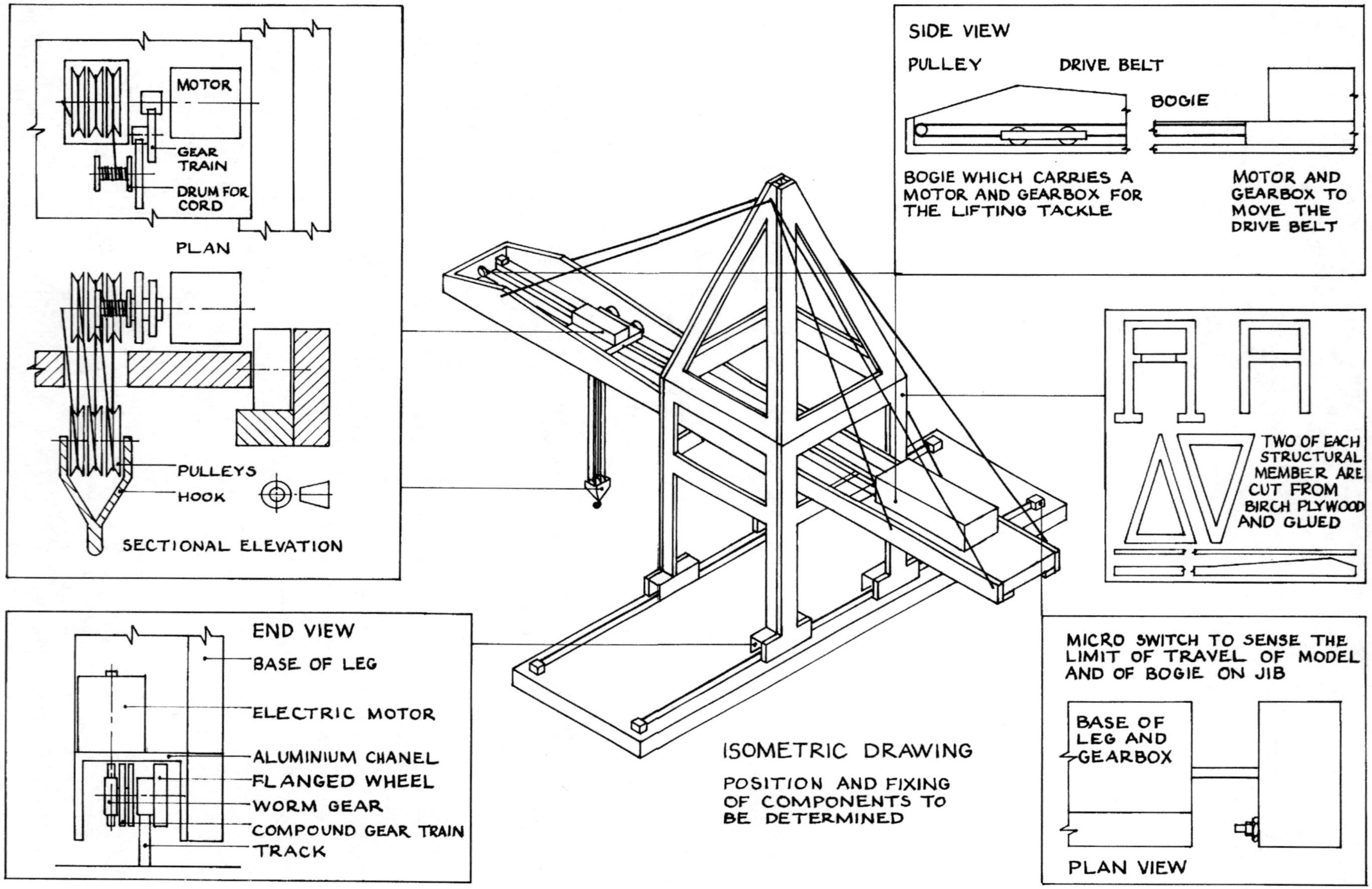

MOTOR

GEAR TRAIN

DRUM FOR CORD

PLAN

PULLEYS

HOOK

SECTIONAL ELEVATION

END VIEW

BASE OF LEG

ELECTRIC MOTOR

ALUMINIUM CHANEL

FLANGED WHEEL

WORM GEAR

COMPOUND GEAR TRAIN

TRACK

Warehousing robot 10

The task

To design and make a prototype, automatically guided, robot buggy.

Task setting

In many warehouses and automated factories, goods and materials need to be moved around efficiently, safely, and quickly and with minimum implied costs. The design should consider various methods of guiding robotic devices and how the electronics involved can be interfaced with the mechanical aspects of the design. Thought may also be given to incorporating collision avoidance, space restrictions, turning circles and 'fail safe' systems.

The aims of the task

- to reinforce the technique of electronic design through a systems approach with an understanding of feedback
- to investigate various types of sensing devices and circuits
- to appreciate the factors involved in interfacing electronics to mechanical devices
- to develop communication skills
- to develop high quality electronic and mechanical making skills.

Values

technical
Students should appreciate the advantages and disadvantages of various methods of driving and steering a robotic device and of sensing position and changes in position.

economic
Students should investigate the financial benefits and liabilities involved with automated systems in manufacturing and distributing goods and materials.

aesthetic
Students should consider the shape and appearance of the real product, bearing in mind where it will be used, who will use it and who will be near it when it is in use.

moral
Students should consider the implications of the introduction of well-designed automated systems into the workplace. Things to think about might include: increased profits, number of people employed, necessary and possible changes in the types of jobs, and skills needed.

social
Students should consider how automated systems can allow people to have more spare time and what they do with that time. They may consider whether or not less working time may mean less income and the social effects of this.

environmental
Students should consider the energy requirements for an automated system against the energy requirements for the same volume of space if worked in by humans. They may also consider the space requirements for storage of materials and goods.

Nature of the product

This is a small, battery-powered, motorized, robot 'buggy' which will automatically follow a track marked on a flat surface or a 'buried' current-carrying wire.

Depending on what type of sensing, electronics, drive system and steering ideas are used, there exists considerable scope for variation and development from the basic device.

Technical knowledge and understanding

- knowledge of methods of driving and steering a robot
- knowledge of suitable sensors (probably opto-electronic sensors but possibly magnetic or capacitive sensors, such as Hall effect and inductive devices, and flat plates connected to very high input impedance devices)
- knowledge and understanding of transistors and operational amplifiers
- knowledge of construction of simple motorized 'platforms'
- knowledge of the manufacture of simple electronic circuits on PCBs.

© The Nuffield Foundation, 1997

Specialist tools, materials and equipment

Each working buggy will require the following:
- a range of electronic components, including transistors, op-amps, light sensors, small filament lamps
- two or three small 6V DC motors (or for more advanced variations, two stepper motors) and gears or pulleys to produce final output of about 60 rpm
- access to prototype boards or systems kits for modelling, investigating and developing possible circuits is useful

- PCB making equipment to produce final circuit
Possible suppliers:
Maplin MPS on 01702 554000
Rapid Electronics on 01206 751166.

Cross-curricular links

maths
- calculations related to potential dividers, current gain, Ohm's law, centre-of-gravity, moments, rotational speed and gear/pulley ratios.

science
- electrical concepts – Ohm's law, current, resistance, potential difference, circuits, power sources
- light concepts – nature of light, intensity and spectral characteristics of light sources
- mechanics concepts – moments, balance, centre-of-gravity, gear ratios.

art
- sketch books exploring the shapes and forms that are contained in industrial items, such as cranes, bulldozers and forklift trucks, could be used to inform the overall aesthetics of the robot buggy.

IT
- Crocodile Clips or similar software for developing circuits, PCB designing software, CAD for designing a motorized platform.

economical and industrial understanding
- students can investigate the costs of employing people in warehouses and the costs involved in heating spaces. They can also investigate space required for storage, for human access and for robot access.

Useful Resource Tasks

To reinforce the technique of electronic design through a systems approach with an understanding of feedback:
- SBRT 1 *Sensing and processing with transistors*
- SBRT 2 *Using a comparator*
- IBRT 1 *Investigating transistor circuits*
- IBRT 2 *Investigating a comparator*
- CCRT 3 *Working with transistors and op-amps.*

To develop communication skills:
- CRT 2 *Communicating ideas to the maker 1*
- CRT 2 *Communicating ideas to the maker 2.*

To develop high quality electronic and mechanical making skills:
- MfRT 3 *Assembling an electromechanical system*
- ECRT 1 *Controlling a simple buggy*
- ECRT 2 *Choosing batteries.*

Useful Case Studies

To reinforce the technique of electronic design through a systems approach with an understanding of feedback:
- Communicating devices – bus arrival times system, the countdown service.

Design brief

To design and make a prototype working model of an automatic means of moving materials and goods around a warehouse or factory. The design should be such that the route taken by the materials can be easily and cheaply changed. The model will be used by sales representatives to demonstrate to possible customers how automatic goods transportation in warehouses and factories could benefit their company.

Preliminary specification

What the product should do:
- be able to follow an easily painted track or guide line or current-carrying wire with at least three bends
- stop automatically when it comes to the end of the track
- stop automatically if it comes off the track.

What the product should look like:
- It should have an appearance in keeping with the working environment and also pleasing to those who work with/near it.

Other features:
- it must run off batteries
- have facilities to replace the batteries

- no part of the device must over-heat
- it must not be guided manually once it has started
- it must not be affected by changes in ambient light.

Possible optional features:
- it should be possible to allow it to take a defined direction at a 'Y' junction in the path with only a simple change to the device (different-coloured tracks could be used here)
- it could sound an alarm if it come off the track or reaches the end
- it could turn round and retrace its path when it reaches the end of the track
- it could stop or change direction if it collides with a fixed object.

Design sketches

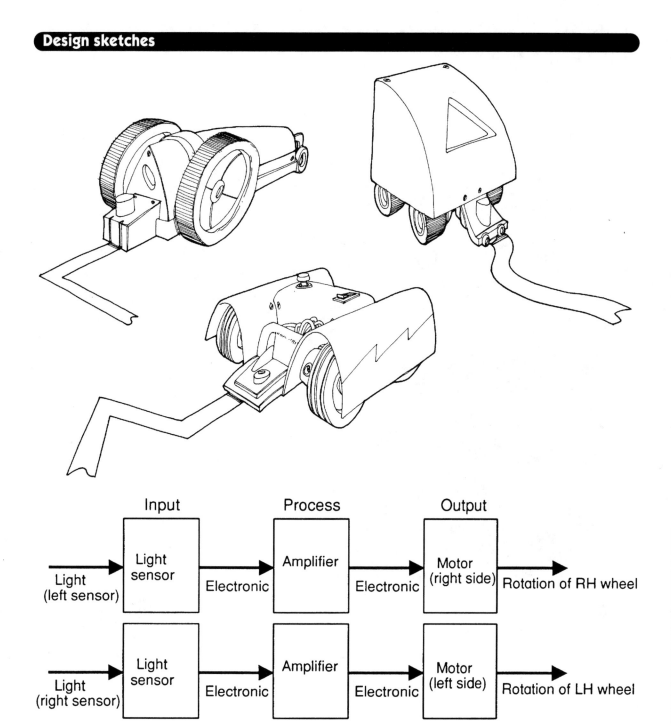

Input	Process	Output	
Light (left sensor) →	Light sensor → Electronic →	Amplifier → Electronic →	Motor (right side) → Rotation of RH wheel
Light (right sensor) →	Light sensor → Electronic →	Amplifier → Electronic →	Motor (left side) → Rotation of LH wheel

Information for making

Likely solution

Left and right turning motors controlled by
the amount of light reaching LDRs mounted
either side of the line to be followed.

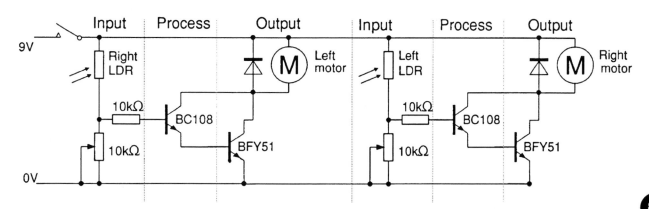

Information for making

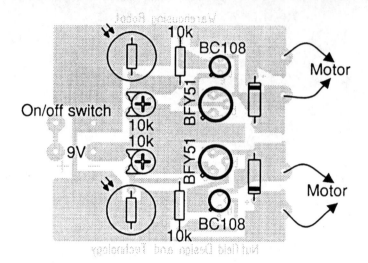

On/off switch

10k

9V

10k

10k

10k

BC108

BFY51

BFY51

BC108

Motor

Motor

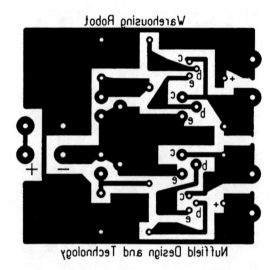

Warehousing Robot

Nuffield Design and Technology

THIRD ANGLE ORTHOGRAPHIC PROJECTION

DRIVEN GEAR 40 TEETH

COMPOUND GEAR 10/30 TEETH

WORM GEAR DRIVER

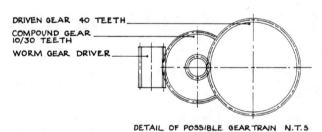

DETAIL OF POSSIBLE GEARTRAIN N.T.S

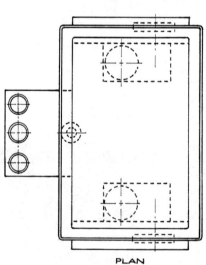

PLAN

VACUUM FORMED PLASTICS TRAY

STRIP BENT PLASTICS BODY SHELL

SHEET MATERIAL CHASSIS

PLASTICS TUBING LDR SHIELD

ELECTRIC MOTOR

SPACE FOR PCB

BENT ALUMINIUM SHEET GEARBOX

PLASTICS TUBING LIGHT SHIELD

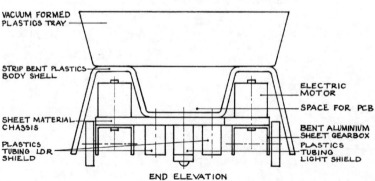

END ELEVATION

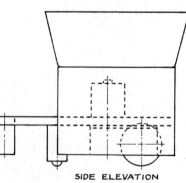

SIDE ELEVATION

Radical radios

A Capability Task for electronics
Line of interest – communication devices

The task

To design and make a radio that is one of a range that are suited for use in a particular situation.

Task setting

There are many occasions when it is useful to listen to the radio, such as:

- at sporting events so that you can hear the commentary as you watch
- while travelling
- while training in a gym
- while in hospital
- while cooking or preparing food
- while studying.

It is possible to develop each situation into a commercial possibility. For example, it is easy to imagine a cardboard returnable radio for use at sporting events where the outer card shell is changed according to the sporting event taking place but the internal workings are reused many times. Spectators simply hire a radio as they enter and return it as they leave. The students' task is to take a situation of their own choosing, where listening to the radio would be useful, and to design and make one of a range of radios suited for that situation. The radios would be mass produced for sale through retail outlets or specialist trade journals.

The aims of the task

- to enable students to identify a situation where using a radio is important
- to enable students to build and adjust a simple radio circuit
- to enable students to develop skills in designing and making a shell for the radio and also a user guide.

Values

technical

Students should consider the advantages and disadvantages of different listening and tuning devices.

economic

Students should appreciate the wide range of economic activity required for radio broadcasting and reception.

aesthetic

Students should design a case for the product, which is appropriate to the purpose of the device and the place where it will be used.

moral

Students should consider the issues involved in broadcasting in terms of honesty, truth and decency.

social

Students should consider the merits of manufacturing products, such as personal radios, which promote solitary and potentially anti-social leisure activity.

environmental

Students should consider the effects of sound from radios causing annoyance and contributing to noise pollution.

Nature of the product

This radio is suited for use in a particular situation. A given radio circuit, such as the TEP FM radio, can be used as the basic circuit. Students can adjust for optimum performance and experiment with different speakers and headsets. The more able student may be encouraged to calibrate the reception dial and develop sensitive tuning mechanisms.

Technical knowledge and understanding

- knowledge of a basic radio circuit (TEP FM or similar)
- knowledge of speakers and headphones
- knowledge of enclosure production techniques.

Specialist tools, materials and equipment

- a basic radio circuit (TEP FM or similar)
- a range of suitable speakers and headphones
  Possible suppliers:
  Teaching Resources, Middlesex University 0181 447 0342
- vacuum forming facilities.

Cross-curricular links

maths
- simple calculations of features such as radio wave length and suitable aerial length.

science
- relevant concepts, such as electromagnetic spectrum, wavelength, frequency, propagation speed, sound waves.

art
- sketch books exploring the relationship between the shapes and forms contained within the situation could be used to inform the overall aesthetics of the radio.

IT
- CAD for designing networks of simple shells; CAM for cutting and creasing card shells.

economic and industrial understanding
- students can investigate the range of commercial and industrial activity related to local radio stations.

Useful Resource Tasks

To enable students to identify a situation where using a radio is important:
- SRT 1 *Identifying needs and likes*
- SRT 5 *Attribute analysis*.

To enable students to develop skills in designing and making a shell for the radio:
- CRT 1 *Communicating ideas to the client*
- MfRT 4 *Producing enclosures*.

To enable students to develop skills in designing and making a user guide:
- CRT 4 *Communicating to the user*.

To enable students to build and adjust a simple radio circuit:
- CTRT 1 *Making and testing a radio (based on the TEP radio)*.

Useful Case Studies

To enable students to identify a situation where using a radio is important:
- Communicating devices – clockwork radio
- A radio revolution.

Design brief

To design and make a radio to be used by a specified person in a particular situation. The appearance should reflect the user and the situation. The radio will be sold at retail outlets such as Dixons or Tandy and through specialist trade journals.

Preliminary specification

What the product should do:
- receive the main advertised FM stations
- produce a sound output via either headphones or a speaker.

What the product should look like:
- suit the purpose of the device
- suit the location in which the product will be used.

Other features:
- how it should work
- be powered from a battery
- have facilities to replace the battery
- meet EU safety requirements.

Design sketches

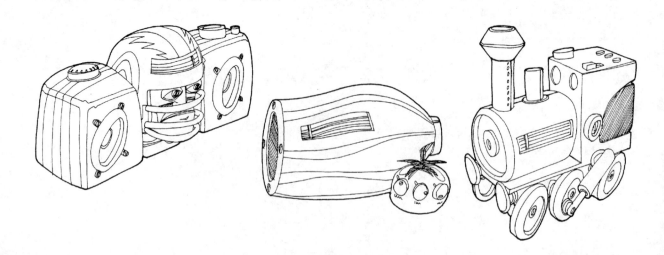

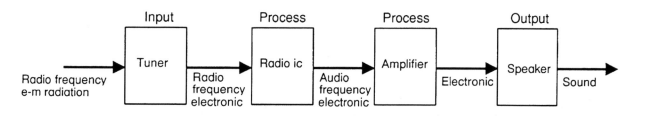

Input	Process	Process	Output
Tuner	Radio ic	Amplifier	Speaker

Radio frequency e-m radiation → Tuner → Radio frequency electronic → Radio ic → Audio frequency electronic → Amplifier → Electronic → Speaker → Sound

Information for making

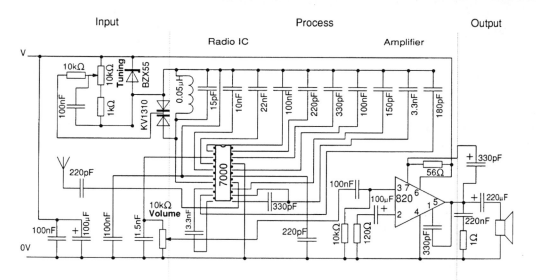

Input — Process — Output

Radio IC — Amplifier

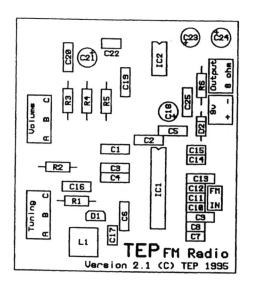

TEP FM Radio
Version 2.1 (C) TEP 1995

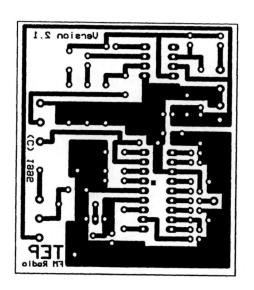

Version 2.1
(C) 1995
TEP FM Radio

Likely solution
A given radio circuit completed and adjusted for optimum performance incorporated into an appropriate casing – either card or plastic – plus sound output via either speakers or headphones.

Basic radio circuit
This can be tuned in to receive FM stations.

Product modification
How would you improve the ease of tuning?

Drawn and cut out using CAD/CAM

Position and fixing of components to be determined

Glue tab

An oblique view of the assembled enclosure

© The Nuffield Foundation, 1997

⑫ Radio control toys

A Capability Task for electronics
Line of interest – communication devices

The task

To design and make a radio control model that is suitable for a particular user.

Task setting

Radio control models provide amusement and enjoyment for a wide range of users; from the young child using an inexpensive, mass-produced simple toy to the adult enthusiast using a costly, handmade, sophisticated scale model requiring considerable skill to operate. The students' task is to identify a user and to design and make a radio control model that meets their leisure requirements.

The aims of the task

- to enable students to identify a user group which might gain enjoyment from using a radio control model
- to enable students to investigate, build and adjust a simple radio control system
- to enable students to develop the mechanical knowledge and skill needed to design and make a radio control model
- to enable students to develop a model with visual appeal.

Values

technical
Students should consider the levels of accuracy needed to achieve precise control.

economic
Students should consider the idea of disposable income and how this is used for leisure activities.

aesthetic
Students should consider the visual appeal of the model in terms of the requirements of the user and the aesthetics inherent in the artefact itself.

moral
Students should consider the nature of toys and how these can influence behaviour.

social
Students should consider the place of leisure activities in a person's social life, particularly the ideas of an enthusiasts' club.

environmental
Students should consider the effects that using radio control models might have on the environment.

Nature of the product

This is a radio control model that is suitable for a particular user. A less able student might disassemble an existing toy and build the receiver, transmitter and servos into a model of their own design. A more able student might build the circuitry from existing plans.

Technical knowledge and understanding

- knowledge of a basic radio control functions – transmission, reception, servo motors
- knowledge of mechanical systems
- knowledge of model making techniques.

Specialist tools, materials and equipment

- disused radio control models
- servo motors
- mechanical components
- rechargeable batteries
- battery charger
  Possible suppliers:
  Maplin MPS on 01702 554000
  Rapid Electronics on 01206 751166
- vacuum forming facilities.

© The Nuffield Foundation, 1997

Cross-curricular links

maths
- simple graphical representation of pulsing and pulse width modulation.

science
- relevant concepts, such as electromagnetic spectrum, wavelength, frequency, propagation speed.

art
- sketches of real artefacts – cars, lorries, boats, etc. – can be simplified to give makeable forms which capture the essence of the artefact.

IT
- CAD for designing networks of simple shells; CAM for cutting and creasing card or thin plastic shells.

economic and industrial understanding
- students should familiarize themselves with the legal requirements for broadcasting in the radio wave spectrum.

Useful Resource Tasks

To enable students to identify a user group which might gain enjoyment from using a radio control model:
- SRT 2 *Questionnaires*
- SRT 4 *Brainstorming*.

To enable students to investigate, a simple radio control system:
- SBRT 3 *Introducing timing into circuits*
- PART 1 *Looking at a single product*.
(This can be adapted to look specifically at simple radio control models.)

To enable students to develop the mechanical knowledge and skill needed to design and make a radio control model:
- MfRT 3 *Assembling an electromechanical system*.

To enable students to develop a model with visual appeal:
- CRT 1 *Communicating ideas to the client*.

Useful Case Studies

To enable students to investigate, a simple radio control system:
- Communicating devices – bus arrival times system, the countdown service

Design brief

To design and make a radio control model that is suitable for a particular user group. The appearance and performance of the model should have general appeal for the specified user group. The radio will be sold at major retail outlets – Dixons, Tandy, Toys Я Us and/or specialist hobby shops.

Preliminary specification

What the product should do:
- operate by means of radio control
- move in an appropriate manner.

What the product should look like:
- have appeal for the specified user group
- be in keeping with the aesthetics of the artefact itself.

Other features:
- be powered from a rechargeable battery
- have facilities to replace the battery
- meet EU safety requirements.

Design sketches

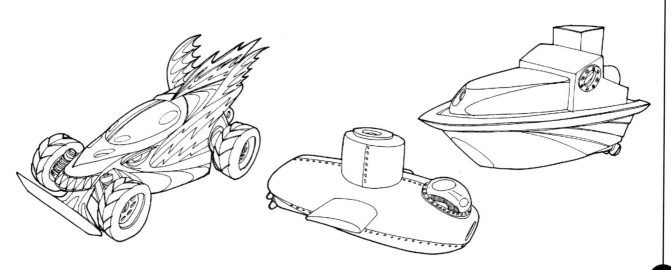

© The Nuffield Foundation, 1997

Transmitter

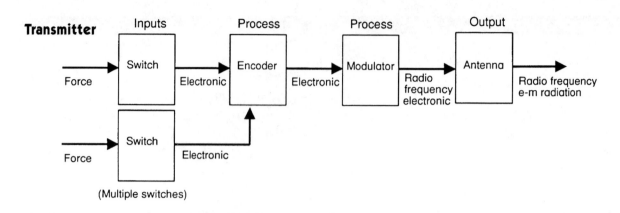

Inputs | Process | Process | Output

Force → Switch → Electronic → Encoder → Electronic → Modulator → Radio frequency electronic → Antenna → Radio frequency e-m radiation

Force → Switch → Electronic

(Multiple switches)

Information for making

Transmitter

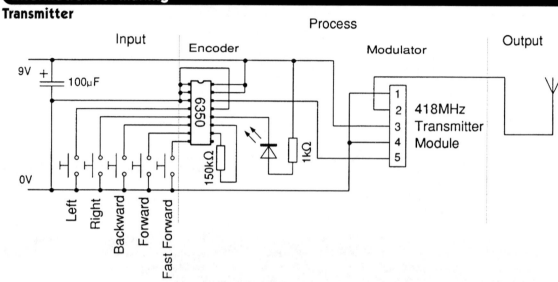

Process

Input | Encoder | Modulator | Output

9V
100μF
6350
150kΩ
1kΩ
0V

Left | Right | Backward | Forward | Fast Forward

1
2
3
4
5
418MHz Transmitter Module

Likely solution
A completed rad[...]
control model in[...]
which the circui[...]
has been either t[...]
from an existing
model or built fr[...]
given circuit
diagrams.

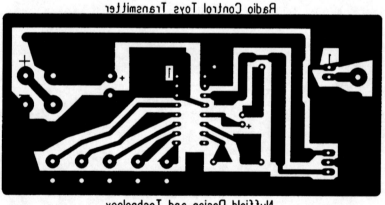

Radio Control Toys Transmitter

Nuffield Design and Technology

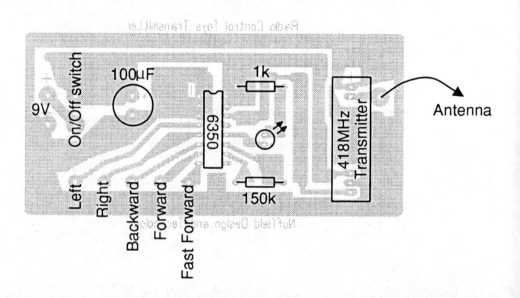

Radio Control Toys Transmitter

9V | On/Off switch | 100μF | 6350 | 1k | 150k | 418MHz Transmitter | Antenna

Left | Right | Backward | Forward | Fast Forward

Nuffield Design and Technology

Design sketches
Receiver

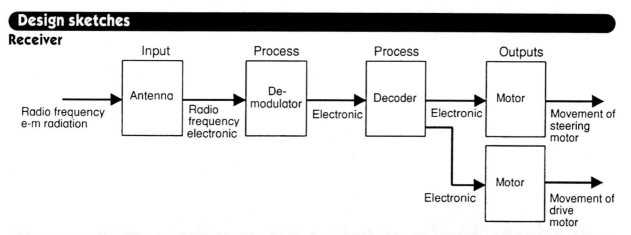

Information for making
Receiver

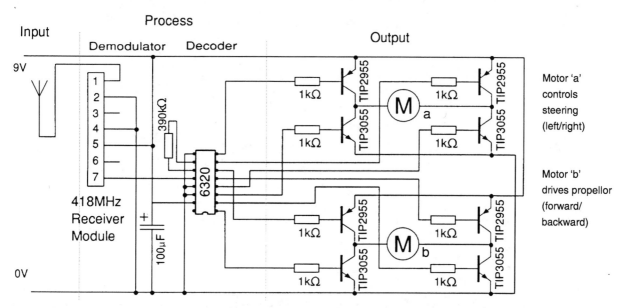

These circuits make use of a matched pair of 418MHz modules made by Radiometrix. These are widely available (e.g. from Maplin). The data sheet that accompanies them gives full information on their use and on constructing suitable antennae for them. The matched pair of encoder/decoder ICs (6350/6320) are designed especially for model control. Again there is a data sheet detailing all of their functions.

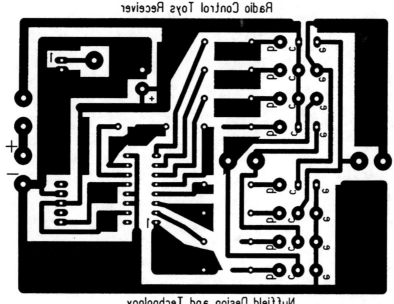

Information for making
Receiver

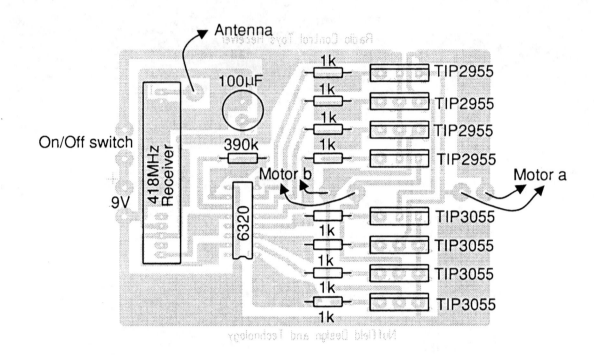

Antenna
100µF
On/Off switch
418MHz Receiver
9V
6320
390k
1k
1k
1k
1k
1k
1k
1k
1k
1k
TIP2955
TIP2955
TIP2955
TIP2955
TIP3055
TIP3055
TIP3055
TIP3055
Motor b
Motor a

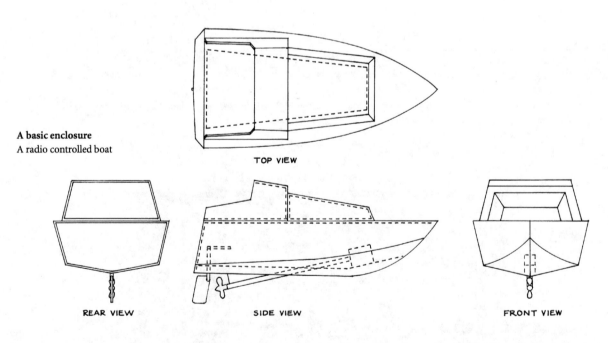

A basic enclosure
A radio controlled boat

TOP VIEW

REAR VIEW   SIDE VIEW   FRONT VIEW

THIRD ANGLE ORTHOGRAPHIC DRAWING

CONSTRUCTED FROM THIN
SHEET MATERIAL SUCH AS
CARD, PLYWOOD, BALSA
OR PLASTIC, GLUED WITH
WATERPROOF ADHESIVE.
POSITION AND FIXING OF
COMPONENTS TO BE DETER-
MINED

A Capability Task for electronics
Line of interest – multiple line products

The task

To design and make a prototype buggy that can survive a parachute landing, travel, use sensors to capture data and then transmit that data to a central receiving station.

Task setting

Most industrial research and development activity is carried out by teams of people, each person contributing a specialist discipline. The Mars Lander task provides the opportunity for a group of able students to work together in this way. The task can be divided into a series of related sub-tasks:

- chassis and wheels/tracks design
- drive system design
- drive transmission system design
- data collection system design
- encoding and decoding system
- transmission and reception system design.

The outcomes of all of these sub-tasks have to be interfaced with each other in the production of a prototype buggy.

This is an ambitious task and it will require the students to acquire knowledge and skill well beyond that normally needed for GCSE D&T (electronic products). It is, however, a worthwhile and challenging activity that could be carried out, in part, in an out of school club.

The aims of the task

- to enable students to work in a multidisciplinary team
- to enable students to acquire new technical knowledge and skills
- to enable students to develop a complex multifunctional technical system.

Values

technical

Students should consider the levels of knowledge and skill needed to achieve satisfactory design solutions.

economic

Students should consider the cost and benefits of ambitious technological endeavours such as visiting other planets.

aesthetic

Sudents should consider the visual appeal of the prototype and the aesthetics inherent in the artefact itself.

moral

Students should consider the justification for interplanetary travel and exploration.

social

Students should consider the impact of space travel on the way we see ourselves.

environmental

Students should consider the possible impact of exploration on remote places.

Nature of the product

A prototype, small-scale buggy that can survive a parachute landing and move around its surroundings, collecting data which it transmits to a remote reception centre.

Technical knowledge and understanding

- knowledge of transmission and reception systems
- knowledge of data gathering systems
- knowledge of microcontrollers
- knowledge of encoding and decoding systems
- knowledge of mechanical systems
- knowledge of electrical systems
- knowledge of model making techniques.

Specialist tools, materials and equipment

- a useful starting point is transmitter/receiver modules supplied as self-assembly kits by Maplin MPS (01702 554000).
- microcontrollers can be obtainer from Teaching Resources, Middlesex University (0181 447 0342) and ICON Project Nottingham Trent University
- vacuum forming facilities.

© The Nuffield Foundation, 1997

Cross-curricular links

maths
- relevant concepts, such as devising instructions to produce desired movements along a path, data handling, using vectors.

science
- relevant concepts, such as electromagnetic spectrum, wavelength, frequency, propagation speed.

IT
- For data gathering.

art
- sketches of real, tough-terrain land vehicles – tanks, dune buggies, jeeps – can be simplified to give makeable forms which can be used to develop the appearance of the buggy.

economic and industrial understanding
- students should consider the funding sources for long-term research and development.

Useful Resource Tasks

Students will need to have tackled most of the following Resource Tasks as a precursor to work on the Mars Lander:
- ECRT 1 *Controlling a simple buggy*
- SBRT 1 *Sensing and processing with transistors*
- SBRT 2 *Using a comparator*
- SBRT 3 *Introducing timing into circuits*
- SBRT 4 *Combining signals*
- SBRT 5 *Circuits that count*
- IBRT 1 *Investigating transistor circuits*
- IBRT 2 *Investigating a comparator*
- IBRT 3 *Designing timing circuits*
- IBRT 4 *Designing logic circuits*
- IBRT 5 *Investigating counting*
- MfRT 3 *Assembling an electromechanical system*
- CTRT 1 *Making and testing a radio* (based on the TEP radio)
- PICRT 1 *Using microcontrollers*
- PICRT 2 *Comparing simple programmable and hard-wired systems*
- PICRT3 *Developing sophisticated systems.*

Useful Case Studies

To enable students to develop a complex multifunctional technical system:
- Communicating devices – bus arrival times system, the countdown service
- Helping to keep air breathable.

Design brief

To design and make a prototype buggy that can survive a parachute landing, travel, use sensors to capture data and then transmit that data to a central receiving station. Although the buggy is a one-off production, it should be well finished, with considerable aesthetic appeal.

Preliminary specification

What the product should do:
After a parachute landing the buggy should:
- move across the immediate terrain
- capture data about the environment - temperature, light level, humidity, atmospheric contents perhaps
- transmit the data to a central receiving station
- move in an appropriate mannner.

What the product should look like:
- have visual appeal
- be in keeping with the aesthetics of the artefact itself.

Other features:
- be powered from a rechargeable battery
- have facilities to replace the battery.

Design sketches

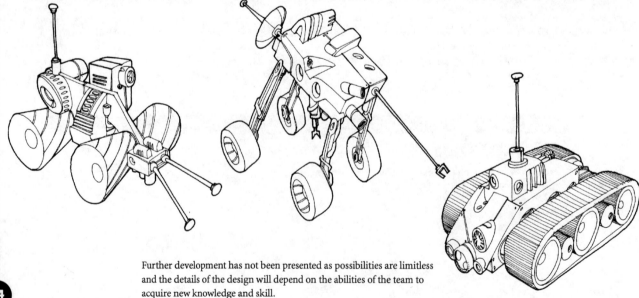

Further development has not been presented as possibilities are limitless and the details of the design will depend on the abilities of the team to acquire new knowledge and skill.